Poetry Mo...

Co Durham
Edited by Steve Twelvetree

 Young**Writers**

First published in Great Britain in 2004 by:
Young Writers
Remus House
Coltsfoot Drive
Peterborough
PE2 9JX
Telephone: 01733 890066
Website: www.youngwriters.co.uk

All Rights Reserved

© *Copyright Contributors 2004*

SB ISBN 1 84460 351 2

Foreword

This year, the Young Writers' 'Poetry In Motion' competition proudly presents a showcase of the best poetic talent selected from over 40,000 up-and-coming writers nationwide.

Young Writers was established in 1991 to promote the reading and writing of poetry within schools and to the youth of today. Our books nurture and inspire confidence in the ability of young writers and provide a snapshot of poems written in schools and at home by budding poets of the future.

The thought effort, imagination and hard work put into each poem impressed us all and the task of selecting poems was a difficult but nevertheless enjoyable experience.

We hope you are as pleased as we are with the final selection and that you and your family continue to be entertained with *Poetry In Motion Co Durham* for many years to come.

Contents

Glendene Special School
Lee Simpson (14)	1
Daniel Sheridan (14)	2
Barry Young (13)	2
Vicky Malkin (14)	3

Hummersknott Comprehensive School
Laura Raine (11)	3
Andrew Kelly (11)	4
Laura Thompson (11)	4
Reanne Donnison (11)	4
Joanne Fishburn	5
Megan Bartle (12)	5
Lucy Madden (14)	6
Sophie Madden (11)	7
Elliot Kent (12)	7
Sarah Nicholson	8
Taran Draper	8
Amanda Jackson (12)	9
Hannah Kattou (11)	9
Jarred Harper (11)	10
Neil Mallaby (12)	10
Debbie Theakston	10
Craig Mallaby	11
Chloe Iles (11)	11
Laura Banham (12)	12
Dan Gordon	12
Jenny Atkinson (12)	13
Hayley Gault	13
Melissa Cradock (13)	14
Jamie Mitchinson (11)	14
Tom Page (11)	15
Laura Craven (12)	15
Adam Shield (11)	16
Conor Gower	17
Alex Hutchinson (11)	17
Chloe Hull	17
Andrew Grainger (12)	18
Hannah Brough (11)	18

Faye Broadbent (11)	19
Andrew White	19
Katherine Dawson (12)	20
Lee Soanes (13)	20
Fiona Metcalfe (12)	21
Andrew Finn	21
Morgan Edwards (12)	22
Victoria Walker (11)	22
Bridgette Crozier (12)	23
Carl Fitz-Gerald	23
Samantha Lawrence	24
Stephanie Hogg (11)	24
Mark Woodward	25
Sarah Nicholson (12)	25

Hurworth Maths & Computing College

Natalie Rowbottom (12)	26
Nicky Gardner (12)	26
Ami Walker & Tanya Atkinson (15)	27
Conrad Jackson (12)	27
Christopher Barnard (12)	28
Laura Booth (12)	28
Daniel Arkle (13)	29
Yasmine Merriott (13)	29
Carl Jameson (12)	30
Bobbie Sewell (12)	30
Adam Sturgeon (13)	31
Clare Rudd (12)	31
Robyn Simpson (12)	32
Sophie Tedd (12)	32
Ashleigh Atkinson (12)	33
Jordan Atkinson (12)	33
Adam Wright (13)	34
Kathryn Parker (13)	34
Youssef Mahmoud (14)	35
Emma Brentley (12)	35
Leah Foley (13)	36
Katherine Hobson (13)	36
Jamie Myers (12)	36
Beth Frankland (12)	37
Megan Hall (13)	37

Ben Harper (12)	38
Vicky Moffatt (13)	38
Paul Dees (13)	39
Laura Bennett (13)	40
Alix Leach (14)	40
Rohanna Aston (13)	41
Emma Walton (13)	42
Katie Bearpark (13)	42
Rebekah Brydon (14)	43
James Walton (13)	43
Robbie Gardner (13)	44
Oliver Chapman (13)	45
Amy Ralph (13)	45
Matthew Phillips (13)	46
Chris Barron (13)	47
Rachel Metcalfe (12)	48
Louise Foley (13)	48
Lauren Hume (13)	49
Adam Hassan (13)	49
Gemma Arnold (13)	50
Stacey Hodgson (13)	51
Jennifer Mitchell (12)	51
Clare Peacock (15)	52
Claire Todd (15)	52
Romeela Rana-Rahman (15)	53
Laura Dillon (15)	54
Rebecca Boyd (13)	54
Kirsty Williamson (13)	55
Shaun Marshall (13)	55
Jessica Harris (13)	56
Clare Holme (13)	56
Lauren Mitchell (13)	57
Daniel Sutcliffe (13)	57
Neneh Kaur Binning (13)	58
Chris Lapping (13)	59
Pav Toor (13)	60
Clare Eddy (12)	60
Jack Dell (13)	61
Robert Edwards (13)	62
Gemma Baker (12)	62
Nichola Bateman (12)	63
Nathaniel Merriott (12)	63

Daniel Gayles (12) 64
Paris Lowcock (12) 64
Stephanie Leonard (12) 65
Matthew Smith (12) 65
Catherine Brown (13) 66
Jonathan Weeks (12) 67
Sabriye Wallis (12) 67
Craig Peacock (12) 68
Becky Mullett (12) 68
Francesca Heath (12) 69

Lord Lawson of Beamish School
David Robbins (11) 69
Victoria Routledge (11) 70
James Welsh (11) 70
Billy Harwood (11) 71
Ben Taylor (11) 71
David Talbot (12) 71
Nicole Sharkey (11) 72
Alex Bills (11) 72
Laura Charlton (11) 73
Kyle Davie (11) 73
Matthew Jennings (11) 74
Lauren Turner (11) 74
Paul Old (11) 75
Abby Kelford (12) 75
Liam Hall (11) 76
Holly Nevin (11) 76
Danny Riley (11) 76
Christopher Tiffin (11) 77
Kayleigh Trainer (11) 77
Callum Russell (11) 78

Moorside Community College
Rachel Hodgson (12) 78
Matthew Nash (15) 79
Jason Barsby (12) 79
Lauren Dyer (12) 80
Amber Cranson (12) 80
Kaye Lowery (15) 81
Richard Walford (15) 81

Lynsey Davison (15)	82
Gilly Nelson (13)	82
Shaun Connolly (15)	83
Kate Cranson (12)	83
Lea Griffiths (15)	84
Levi Taylor (12)	84
Paul Clarke (15)	85
Caroline Slater (15)	85
Andrew Lee (15)	86
Katie Affleck (12)	86
Laura McGregor (15)	87
Lauren Robinson (12)	87
Caroline Wyatt (14)	88
Emma Bramley (12)	88
Rachel Drury (14)	89
Marc Milburn (12)	89
Alex Milburn (14)	90
Helen Woodward (13)	90
Annette Simpson (12)	91
Pearl-Susanne Davison (12)	91
Sarah Louise Bridgewater (14)	92
Kimberley Walton (14)	92
Kimberley Stephenson (12)	93
Steven Livingstone (14)	93
Steven Clarke (14)	94
Lee Smith (14)	94
Leanne Bullamore (14)	94
David Stephenson (14)	95
Rebecca Grant (14)	95
Jasmine Glasgow (14)	95
Lauren Webster (14)	96
Kathryn Tyler (14)	96
Gareth Ferguson (14)	97
Danielle Albon (13)	97
Gemma Lister (14)	97

Polam Hall School

Jessica Robb (14)	98
Suzie Millar (11)	99
Rachel Alban (13)	100
Kristina Gallagher (13)	101

Roseberry Sports & Community College

Ashleigh Williams (12)	101
Mark Lynn (12)	102
Laura Pearson (12)	102
Sarah-Lee Gordon Pearse (12)	103
Laura Ames (12)	103
James Gibbs (13)	104
Lyndsey Brown (13)	104
Sophie Short (11)	105
Marie Forster (12)	105
Natasha Jayne Scott (12)	106
Jennifer Anderson (11)	106
Chloe Williams (11)	107
Natalie Duncan (12)	107
Anna Widdrington (11)	107
Kate Atkinson (11)	108
Alex Young (11)	108
Andrew Lough (13)	109
Yasmine Khalifa (14)	110
Natalie Thompson (13)	110
Brian Ashman (13)	111
Paul Hunt (13)	111
Thomas Owers (13)	112
Dayne Nicholson (14)	112
Scott Harrison (13)	113
Lauren Bates (13)	113
Kayleigh Worrall (13)	114
Laura McFarling (11)	114
Helen Shaw (13)	115
Callum McCutcheon (11)	115
Callum Sharpe (12)	116
Jack Norwood (11)	117
Rebecca Simpson (11)	117
Justine Ovington (12)	118
Chloe Miles (11)	118
Gemma Piggford (11)	119
Benjamin Brown (12)	119
Emma Wilson (12)	120
Stephnie Coyle (13)	120
Matthew Gray (11)	121
Ashleigh McCluskey-Walke (11)	121
Scott Docherty (11)	122

Kristina Stafford (11)	123
Anna Jobling (11)	123
Kristie Armstrong (12)	124
Laura Alderson (11)	124
Jasmine Mulligan (12)	125
Rachel Campbell (12)	125
Ben Johnson (12)	126
Chris Smith (12)	126
Christopher Bevan (12)	127
Carley Cockburn (12)	127
Kimberley Bell (12)	128
Ryan Mowbray (11)	128
Daynor Dockery (12)	129
Natalie Barker (11)	129
Sally Hunter (13)	130
Donna Ashurst (12)	130
Matthew Soulsby (11)	131
Carl Gill (12)	131
Daniel Ross (11)	132
Ashton Carter Ridgway (11)	132
Katie Pearson (12)	133
Abigail Forster (11)	133
Holly Tallentire (12)	134
Daniel Howe (11)	134
Paul William Franklin (11)	135
Danielle Graham (11)	135
Sally Ann Rawlinson (12)	136
Jamie Patterson (11)	136
Dale Bruce Purvis (12)	137
Christopher Waistell (11)	137
Stephen Lough (12)	138
Sophie Harkness (11)	138
Stephanie Carr (11)	139
Christopher Twycross (12)	139
James Miller (12)	140
Grant Stephenson (11)	140
Fiona Alyson Lane (12)	141
Tom Charlton (11)	141
Sarah Davison (12)	142
Harriet Middleton (12)	142
Thomas Bates (12)	143
Jonathan Brown (12)	143

Georgia Gibson (12) 144
Sarah Harris (13) 144
Hannah Livesey (12) 145
Lynne Eason (12) 145
Lauren Patterson (11) 146
Michael Miley (13) 147

The Hermitage School
Nicola Hoyle (14) 147
Jake Rollings (15) 148
Kate Pickard 148
Ian Potts (15) 149
Mark Ridley 149
Michael Patterson 150
Christopher Porter (15) 151
Lauren Prout (15) 151
Jonathan Carter (15) 152
Toni Paget 152
Kathryn Louise Rudd (15) 153
Claire Renneberg (14) 154
Emma Hall (15) 154
Andrew Graham (14) 155

The Poems

Golden

A golden moon
Above a golden beach,
A sudden reach
Upon a golden beach,
Golden stones
Upon golden sand.

A golden mountain
Upon a glowing river
Of shiny gold,
By the golden moon
Is shining beams of gold.

Why are the golden trees
Bothered by the busy bees?

When the golden moon has set
Soon the river would have slept.
Through the sleeping fish
The sleeping people would have slept,
But only the golden beach
Would be even greater,
Through the golden sand
And golden stone.

The busy bees should have slept,
Of the golden leaves of the trees.

The golden moon
Has long been set,
So now the sun shall take its place.

Lee Simpson (14)
Glendene Special School

The Circus

The circus is clowns, clowns on stilts
    That tilt.
The circus is lions, lion tamers,
    Arrow aimers.
The circus is trapezes, trapeze noise,
    Clockwork toys.
The circus is tigers, tiger's stares
    And dancing bears.
The circus is circus masters, master's whip
    And dancing tips.
The circus drum, beats,
    Masses of seats.
The circus is hoops of fire,
    And a singing choir.

Daniel Sheridan (14)
Glendene Special School

North East

Do you remember the north east? I do.
Do you remember the north east? I do.
And the tunnels and the funnels
And the pits and the shafts.
Then the raft on the river, that made me quiver.
To the animals in the woods, in the forests and the castles.
Do you remember the north east? I do.
Do you remember the north east? I do.
To the shops on the top of the hill
And the art that is smart in the galleries.
Do you remember the north east? I do.
Do you remember the north east? I do.
From the flowers of the north to the sky of the east
And trains that go round the corners of the railway track
And the people of the past, in the pits and their wheels.

Barry Young (13)
Glendene Special School

Winter Poem

Winter is ice, frosty ice.
Winter is rice, boiled rice.
Winter is gloves, hot gloves.
Winter is doves, snow doves.
Winter is boots, black boots.
Winter is food, Christmas food.
Winter is nights, dark nights.
Winter is lights, northern lights.
Winter is snowballs, water falls.
Winter is snowflakes.
Winter is fairy cakes.
Winter is coats.
Winter is stoats.
Winter is beds
Full of sleepy heads.

Vicky Malkin (14)
Glendene Special School

The Antarctic Penguin

I am a little penguin
In the winter snow
Playing in the cold Antarctic blow

Snow falls all around me
Covering the floor
A cotton wool carpet
For evermore.

The weather is cold and bitter
A sharp and icy wind
I am a little penguin
And now I must go home.

Laura Raine (11)
Hummersknott Comprehensive School

Winter Birds

Winter birds hibernate
As Christmas time comes
Winter birds may see the gate
As humans enjoy winter buns
Winter birds afraid and cold
As humans sit nice and snug
Winter birds die and mould
As humans drink cocoa in their mug.

Andrew Kelly (11)
Hummersknott Comprehensive School

Winter In The Fridge

I open the fridge,
It is covered in frost and ice.
A snowstorm appears behind me,
It's so cold I'm shivering.
I blink and I am in the Antarctic,
Swimming in the Arctic Ocean.
I shut the fridge door
And I'm back in the cool kitchen.

Laura Thompson (11)
Hummersknott Comprehensive School

A Cold Antarctic Poem

On a cold winter's morning,
I step outside, yawning.
I step on the ground,
I look all around
And see the snow
And the chilly winds blowing.

Reanne Donnison (11)
Hummersknott Comprehensive School

Who I Am

I wake up at 3 o'clock
And set off pushing my block.

I sweat as the sun beats down on me
While the Pharaoh makes everyone flee

I get some water from a fine guard
But never get so much as a spoon full of lard

I carry on my labour throughout the day
And only the servants get their pay

I crave what the Pharaoh now has
I am not rich
This is who I am.

Joanne Fishburn
Hummersknott Comprehensive School

Chocolate

I see the chocolate on the shelf glistening like a jewel.
I pay with a silver coin, the jewel is now mine.

Removing the wrapper carefully
I find neat little squares of chocolate
Like soldiers standing in a row.

I take my first bite, creamy, smooth, rich chocolate
Comes running down my throat.
It tastes like little drops of heaven.

Just one more bite I say to myself.
As if by magic my chocolate has gone.

Megan Bartle (12)
Hummersknott Comprehensive School

Equality?

In the road two children play
    with a ball
        dressed in patched, frayed dungarees
  dirt covering their uncombed hair
        scrapes and bruises on their knees
opposite a tall boy of a similar age
    walks home in his uniform
          from school
the expensive bag swung over his shoulder
    embellished with the logo of the very cool

  An impassable barrier separates them
        invisible to the eyes of youth
but as they grow up and youth fades
    they'll begin to see the harsh truth
  so close and yet worlds apart

    Suddenly the ball is kicked
        by a bare foot
  it glides steadily over the road
        and like a knife the ball cuts
through the barrier their play thing passes
    to stop at the well-shod feet
of the smart boy in the crimson blazer
    so elegant and neat

  For a second they gaze longingly
    in silent disbelief and awe
to the greater promise of life
    they have opened the door
  The moment unites them all
    in the empty promise of equality
like words written in the sand
    that are washed away by the sea
    engulfed by the endless tides
        of this democracy.

Lucy Madden (14)
Hummersknott Comprehensive School

Why?

The flames lick at the buildings,
Rubble everywhere,
Why?
Crackling, spitting fire
Heat, colour burning bright,
Why?
Mother, Nan, gone forever,
My heart aches,
Why?
Friends, family, all life wiped out
Never to return
Why?
Misery, grief,
I have no tears left to cry
Why?
I'm all alone
Why?

Sophie Madden (11)
Hummersknott Comprehensive School

Gone Forever

A burning wreck.
A silent, sad scene.
A ghost town.
A place of memories.
A land of devastation.
A decimated mess.
A dead land.
An empty town.
A great village in flames.
A once wonderful place
Gone forever.

Elliot Kent (12)
Hummersknott Comprehensive School

Alone

Alone
Where are they?
I can see, everything is gone, everywhere is empty.
I can hear, fiery flames, spurting, crackling, burning
My ears are ringing
I can't breathe . . .

Alone
I can smell the smoke, I breathe in
I'm choking
I gasp for air
There is no air
Where is it . . . ?

Alone
Where am I?
I need someone to talk to, to help me, to hold
Where are they?
Where are they?
I am alone . . .

Sarah Nicholson
Hummersknott Comprehensive School

School

When you arrive at school in the morning,
You know the day will be boring,
When you walk through the gate
And lose all faith,
That you'll like that day and stop yawning.

Taran Draper
Hummersknott Comprehensive School

My New Baby Brother

M y new baby brother
Y ells all night

N ever shuts up, unless he's feeding
E verything he does gets attention
W ow, he's spilling his food.

B other, he's nothing but bother
A ll he does is sleep and feed and
B rings up his food on my new top
Y ells and screeches and screams and cries.

B rothers, who wants them?
R orie he is called, what a name
O liver, that is what I wanted to call him
T oys that are mine are now his
H urry up and grow will you
E ven though I really hate him I also
R eally love him.

Amanda Jackson (12)
Hummersknott Comprehensive School

My First Day At Hummersknott

On my first day at Hummersknott School,
I thought it would be kinda cool.
I went into the gates and saw all my mates,
We all went into the hall and saw a man who was very tall.
He took us round to the school
Which was very big
And I thought to myself, *I shouldn't be here,
I'm only a kid.*

Hannah Kattou (11)
Hummersknott Comprehensive School

Cold Place

A very cold place
A very snowy, cold place
A very windy, snowy, cold place
A very freezy, windy, snowy, cold place
An Eskimo eating in a freezy, windy, snowy, cold place
An Eskimo eating snow cones
In a freezy, windy, snowy, cold place.

Jarred Harper (11)
Hummersknott Comprehensive School

Struggling In The Blizzard

It is freezing with snow
I have been walking for miles
I need something warm to carry on
All I can see is snow and ice
The blizzard's getting heavier and faster
My cheeks are going white, I've fainted.

Neil Mallaby (12)
Hummersknott Comprehensive School

The Little Polar Bear

I'm a little polar bear,
In the Arctic winter snow,
Playing with my polar bear friends,
Laughing in the windy blow.
I am a little polar bear playing in the snow.

Debbie Theakston
Hummersknott Comprehensive School

Dream World

Paradise is a world
You always hope to be
Maybe on your own
Or with plenty of company

The sunshine over mountains
The rainbow over trees
The gods you have to worship
When you get down on your knees

But in this land it's not perfect
Guns and bombs for war
Soldiers trying to save the world
So we suffer no more

As I look out the window
I look up in the sky
Some place I thought I'd want to be
The place to rest when I die.

Craig Mallaby
Hummersknott Comprehensive School

My Cold Poem

Ice over water sparkling in the cold,
A house nearby waiting to be sold,
Children trying to be snuggled up in their dorm,
Cats and dogs inside keeping warm,
Warming up by the fire, the adults watch TV,
But I've got central heating, lucky, lucky me!

Chloe Iles (11)
Hummersknott Comprehensive School

Cold

In the Arctic with the ice and snow
Cold waters ripple and chilling winds blow
Penguins waddle on big yellow feet
While others snooze in the snow and sleet
Polar bears lumber noisily around
Their footsteps marking the snowy ground
But the cold is getting to be an issue
Because I have to say *atishoo!*

Laura Banham (12)
Hummersknott Comprehensive School

Play Time

Play time, I love it.
You get to run around,
Play football
And really just mess around.
Play time, I love it.

You've just finished a lesson,
You rush outside,
Ah, fresh air,
You find your mates
And mess around.
Play time, I love it.

It's coming to the end now,
Everyone's having their last kick,
Some are heading for the door,
I wish I could stay out longer.
Play time, I really do love it!

Dan Gordon
Hummersknott Comprehensive School

Animals

Monkeys jump and swing in trees,
Dogs scratch at their itchy fleas.
Tortoises go at their own slow pace,
While hens lay eggs in the same old place.
Pigs like to roll in the mud
And cheetahs run as fast as they should.

Animals are different in lots of ways,
They all have a way of spending their days.

Jenny Atkinson (12)
Hummersknott Comprehensive School

The Whale

I am the beautiful blue whale
Largest not smallest of all.
I thrash in the water
Like a giant beach ball.

I dive in the deep and dark
Fearing no enemy, not even a shark
I roam the sea like a good shark should.

When I swim past the fish they move out of the way
They let me pass, as though I am royal.

I travel for miles, night and day
From winter till spring which is in May
Past all the world in the sea.

'Oh yeah!' I have heard people say
I am the king of the sea.
Well I suppose it's true
Because sharks and fish flee when they see me.
Oh well I think I'll enjoy being
The king of the sea!

Hayley Gault
Hummersknott Comprehensive School

Why Am I Different?

Why am I different God?
What have I done wrong?
Why did you choose me Lord?

I am sure I have always been good,
I have never stolen, hurt or killed,
Please tell me, what I have done wrong Lord?
I'm sure I can put it right.

I can never go out and play,
Feel the sand beneath my toes,
Or go on a bike and feel the wind in my hair.
Please tell me, what I have done wrong Lord?
I'm sure I can put it right.

People treat me differently,
Think I'm something special.
Doctors are my friends,
Children avoid me,
Please tell me, what I have done wrong Lord?
I'm sure I can put it right.

Why am I different Lord?

Melissa Cradock (13)
Hummersknott Comprehensive School

It's Finally Here

Christmas is here
Santa is near
His Christmas sack is full
This year is definitely going to be dull.

There is lots of snow
It looks like a big glow
On the Christmas tree there are lots of lights
But Santa's here, it's alright.

Jamie Mitchinson (11)
Hummersknott Comprehensive School

The Storm

The storm is here,
It fills the people's hearts with fear,
As night sweeps in the storm draws near,
The storm is here.

Like a giant breath the gale begins,
The trees surrender, the gale wins,
Leaves spin and fly around,
Bins spill rubbish and it leaves the ground.

Rain jets hard on the town,
In sheets it swirls, a silver gown,
A car shoots by the empty roads,
Headlights frowning it turns and goes.

The storm then lifts,
The black night shifts,
Back into day again,
Don't ask me why but England's one for rain!

Tom Page (11)
Hummersknott Comprehensive School

Winter

I get dressed up, warm and dry,
Get my sledge, build a snowman way up high.
I start to walk, I start to run,
Playing in the snow is so much fun.
I dance on the ground throwing snowballs in the air,
Although it's freezing, I don't really care.
I like making angels and messing about,
I'm so excited, I just have to shout.

Laura Craven (12)
Hummersknott Comprehensive School

Unappetising School Dinners

School dinners are not food,
You couldn't call it that.
They seem to do nothing except
Make your body very fat.

The chips sit on my plate
Looking green, mushy and bad.
I knew I shouldn't have bought them,
I wish I never had.

The burger's lying there
Looking like Grandpa's feet.
I lift up a slice of 'bread',
Where on earth is the meat?

You couldn't call it a drink,
It has little bits of hair
Swirling around inside,
That's enough to scare.

The peas and carrots alike
Don't deserve a look,
Whoever made these rotten things
Certainly cannot cook.

It really isn't steak,
Its size is just too small.
I go and lift up the school phone
And make to home a call.

My mum comes into school
And brings in a packed lunch.
Finally something good to eat,
I chew it; munch, munch, munch.

Adam Shield (11)
Hummersknott Comprehensive School

Autumn

Autumn trees blow in the wind,
Leaves fall,
And leaves get binned,
Winds get strong,
Nights get long,
Leaves go brown,
And whisk through the town.

Conor Gower
Hummersknott Comprehensive School

The Sea

The sea,
What a wonderful place to be,
The sea ripples forward
Like sea horses skipping waves,
Children happily paddling,
Building sandcastles on the beach,
Time stands still as the sun blazes down,
The sea, what a relaxing place to be.

Alex Hutchinson (11)
Hummersknott Comprehensive School

Christmas

C hristmas is so fun, especially at night,
H ouse is so warm and the fire is bright.
R udolph and Santa are on their way.
I really want to see them on their sleigh.
S now, oh snow, it's snowing outside.
T he windows are rattling, I can't wait to get a surprise.
M y brother comes up and says, 'Look at this.'
A nd my dad comes up and says, 'Make a wish.'
S oon he went so I went back to bed.

Chloe Hull
Hummersknott Comprehensive School

Spider Mania

The depths of the night before a brand new day,
Spiders come to think and play,
Around the garden they scamper and dart,
Spiders are running, they really are smart.

The middle of the night and all is still,
Except a spider's temper ready to spill,
He could blow his top and let anger thrill,
But the name of this spider is Calm Old Bill.

The little ones run and race about,
Some of them having a fun fight bout,
Up and down the old stone wall,
Until their mothers come and call.

The mothers chatter and natter as they do,
Talking about their manly crew,
Thinking about the ones lost down the loo,
Thinking about their manly crew, that is what they do.

Andrew Grainger (12)
Hummersknott Comprehensive School

Summer

  S ummer sun everywhere
  U nderneath the garden chair
  M idges dance here and there
  M um's asleep, what a treat
  E veryone goes out to play
  R un around, laugh all day.

Hannah Brough (11)
Hummersknott Comprehensive School

Evacuation

Going away.
Going away.
Today is a very mournful day.

Everything was fine until
he came
and ruined everything.

The children stood
with their little grey hats
waiting and waiting to leave,
their suitcases packed as they
waved goodbye to all
their families.

Where was I about to go?
Leave my loved ones behind.
I looked out the window and
all I saw were crowds of
sad faces.

I cried and cried but no one answered.
The children screamed, it pierced my ears
but no one answered.

Going away.
Going away.
Today is a very mournful day.

Faye Broadbent (11)
Hummersknott Comprehensive School

A Winter Haiku

As big as a bear
All alone in the Arctic
Follows his mate's tracks.

Andrew White
Hummersknott Comprehensive School

All Year Race

The four racers all line up
Tension is mounting
Winter, Spring, Summer and Autumn,
It's first of January - the race is starting

January straight into February twist
Winter joyfully leads
March surprise and April spin
As Spring speeds

Round May as June and July meet
Summer celebrates
August before September straight
Autumn overtakes

October, into November brake
Autumn and Winter fight
December slide
Winter wins in delight

It's all over as they cross the line
Autumn sulks in disgrace
Summer and Spring cheer
Whilst Winter has a smile on his face.

Katherine Dawson (12)
Hummersknott Comprehensive School

Ebenezer

There once was a man called Ebenezer,
Who was an old smelly geezer.
He was lonely and cruel,
Ate lots of gruel,
Good job he turned out to be an old teaser.

Lee Soanes (13)
Hummersknott Comprehensive School

The Graveyard

In the graveyard
there was a ghost.
In the ghost
there was a spirit.
In the spirit
there was a past life.
In the past life
there was joy.
In the joy
there was a smile.
In a smile
There were teeth.
In the teeth
There were bacteria.
In the bacteria
there were dark monsters

and where do they come from . . . ?

The graveyard.

Fiona Metcalfe (12)
Hummersknott Comprehensive School

The Lonely Dragon

Sitting lonely in his cave,
Crying on the inside,
Fiery on the outside,
Protecting his gold for dear life.

No one even knows him,
However they still try to kill him,
They are throwing spears,
While he is shedding tears.

The lonely dragon.

Andrew Finn
Hummersknott Comprehensive School

Mud

Splish, splosh, splash

Chris making mud cakes
Flying through the air

Splish, splosh, splash

Matty being baked
By the sun, bare

Splish, splosh, splash

Andy doing dive-bombs
In the great mudbath

Splish, splosh, splash

Anna being delicate
Sitting on a chair

Splish, splosh, splash

Amber choosing what to wear
Everyone having fun in the mud.
Morgan Edwards (12)
Hummersknott Comprehensive School

Autumn

Autumn is when leaves start to fall,
Autumn is when the trees are bare,
Autumn starts off the dark nights.

Autumn is when the animals start to hibernate,
Autumn is when conkers start to fall,
Autumn is when flowers start to sleep.
Victoria Walker (11)
Hummersknott Comprehensive School

My Song

I ran away,
So I could play,
But the day is ever so long,
So I sing my song.

Why can't I sing today?
I just want to play.

I strum on my guitar
But it sounds bizarre
Won't someone help me today
So I can play?

Why won't you help me?
No one understands
I just want to play my guitar.

Bridgette Crozier (12)
Hummersknott Comprehensive School

Antarctica Blues

I'm in a cave, no one to show
I'm in as cave, nowhere to go.

Everybody is having a laugh
Where is my friend Cath?

No one is here
What is round the corner, I fear!

I'm in a dark blue, damp cave.

I'm frozen like an iceberg
And there are so many around.

I shiver like an icicle
I shiver on the ground.

I'm still frozen in the dark blue, damp cave.

Carl Fitz-Gerald
Hummersknott Comprehensive School

My Poem

Lost in daytime thoughts
palm tree leaves dancing
in the cool breeze
gushing clear waters
sun burning your skin
a loud bang
the screech of cars
a shiver down your spine
miserable aura
I'm back to reality.

Samantha Lawrence
Hummersknott Comprehensive School

Hallowe'en

Hallowe'en is here at last
It's scary, it's terrifying
Witches, ghosts, devils and vampires
All will be out tonight.

Trick or treat
Go to parties
Have some fun tonight
Get goody bags with your friends.

Some red, some white and some black
Paint your face
Scare people, scare yourself
The scary ghosts will be out tonight.

Get a pumpkin, light it up
Hang it outside
Scare people away
Don't let them come knocking.

Hallowe'en is here at last
It's scary, it's terrifying
Witches, ghosts, devils and vampires
Are you out tonight?

Stephanie Hogg (11)
Hummersknott Comprehensive School

Paradise Poem

I wake up,
I can hear the gentle splash of the sea,
I can smell the sap of the palm trees,
I can see the bright blue morning sky,
I can touch the bright blue morning sky.

My senses return to me,
I can hear the gentle splash of the shower,
I can smell pancakes and honey,
I can see my bright blue walls,
I can touch my blue ceiling.

Yet again,
Another day,
Away from my home.

Mark Woodward
Hummersknott Comprehensive School

A Young Boy's Trade

P urchase a handkerchief
O n the dusty streets of London
C rouched below the long coats
K nees hurting with pain
E ncouraging myself to do it because
T onight I need a place to sleep.

P icking the best pocket
I ensure no one is looking
C ooking up some movement
K eys are in my way
I nside the other dark pocket
N otes are in view so I
G ently slip my hand in and steal.

Sarah Nicholson (12)
Hummersknott Comprehensive School

Lucky

Old, what does it mean?
Hairy, minging, bingo or old sticky toffees,
Nobody knows,
Look at a picture of your gran when she was 4, what do you see?
I see a black and white photo, she is sitting in a chair,
They are the only things in the room,
Shows how lucky I am . . .

A little girl on her own in the street, wearing only a torn shirt,
No money, no food, no water,
Nothing,
I really want to help her, but I don't know how,
She is crying now, she wants her mum,
Shows how lucky I am . . .

When you shout to your mum you want a DVD or a mobile phone
Or even a computer,
If she says no, don't say your life is unfair,
Look how much you have,
A couch and furniture, not just a chair,
A family and home, not just on your own on the street,
You have food and water,
Next time you just think,
I have shown you how lucky you are . . .

Natalie Rowbottom (12)
Hurworth Maths & Computing College

War

War is sad
As well as mad
Those men who died
Were very brave
They fought the fight
With all their might
And now rest in their graves.

Nicky Gardner (12)
Hurworth Maths & Computing College

A Night Out

When the music starts to play,
No one gets in my way
I boogie all night
Till the morning's bright
My feet are burning like balls of fire
As I dance as the music gets higher
My dress swaying side to side
I begin to feel the music inside

I woke up this morning, my head filled with pain
Thinking about the night before, I must be insane
All that dancing and all that wine
Hopefully by the afternoon I will feel fine

Ami Walker & Tanya Atkinson (15)
Hurworth Maths & Computing College

Football

Football is fun to play
So I play it every day
It makes me run around
Sometimes I fall to the ground
When they score a goal
I'm normally the one in the goal
When I get knocked down
I often start to frown
When I get the ball
I quickly pass the ball
I often get hurt
But also get covered in dirt
Then when the game ends
I celebrate with my friends.

Conrad Jackson (12)
Hurworth Maths & Computing College

My Massacre

I walk across my homeland, although the war goes on,
I have only my shield on my arm and my sword in my hand,
I have my brother's blood on my sleeve and my armies' on my leg,
I have no fear of my enemy because I am on my land,
I keep going forward into a living hell,
I point my sword forward and scan the enemies' glory,
I duck the spears of death that fly towards,
I march into the Roman youth, and slice them down,
I hear my captain shout, 'Charge!' as we assault legionaries,
I cut one down and start to fight back against the marching devils,
I then get the pain of a legion's sword into my unguarded side,
I fall to the ground with a great, fearless man's sword in my side,
I had this happen to my father on this land on which I protect,
I see the massacre of men but not as much as I see death.

Christopher Barnard (12)
Hurworth Maths & Computing College

I Am A Vegetarian

I am a vegetarian
I do not like meat
I am not a vegan
As I have a leather seat

I do not like meat
Because the animal sticks in my mind
Each time I try to eat meat
My teeth are unable to grind

My mum doesn't understand
As she always says
'You are designed to eat meat'
On our red days

I don't understand
Why people eat meat
Each animal they kill
It's just another teatime treat.

Laura Booth (12)
Hurworth Maths & Computing College

The Storm

I could taste the salt
as the waves crashed and howled.
The boat just rocked
and people fell flying.

I could hear the wind
as it whistled through my ears.
It became louder and louder
and people drew tears.

I could see the darkness
as there was nothing more to see.
I felt like I was wrapped
by darkness and sea.

I could feel the waves
as they came over me.
They crashed down and spread
and I was sprayed with the sea.

Daniel Arkle (13)
Hurworth Maths & Computing College

The Storm

Waves crash upon the boat
Patches of grey in the sky
Rocking side to side

Huddle up for warmth
Green seas go on and on again
Independence falls

New York seems a dream
Waiting is all we can do
Roaring, fierce storm

Wreckage is floating
Children start to cry and scream
Trapped in a nightmare.

Yasmine Merriott (13)
Hurworth Maths & Computing College

The Croc

The crocodile lay there on the bank
Looking like an armoured tank
His slippy skin is dark and wet
He glides along like a stalking jet

He sees his prey and pounces fast
So his victim cannot last
He chews it round in giant jaws
That seem to be like bolted doors

He leaves a trail wherever he goes
With bits of bones and creatures' toes
Once again he lays in wait
Only to seal another's fate.

Carl Jameson (12)
Hurworth Maths & Computing College

No One Cares, Not A Single Soul

Homeless people, it's so sad,
Staying awake all night.
Children with no dad,
No mum to hold tight.

No one cares, not a single soul,
There is no happiness where they go.
Watching footsteps on the stone floor,
There is no fun, there is just bore.

When I pass them I start to cry,
Do they have friends who care?
Do they have a family or a pet?
No, I don't think so,
Because no one cares, not a single soul.

Bobbie Sewell (12)
Hurworth Maths & Computing College

School Food

The dinner ladies are very rude
And don't get me started about the food
You can find fingernails and hairs
And even worms in the pears
In the gravy there are greenies
And Friday's special is hairy weenies
The sponge and custard makes me sick
And don't remind me about the spotted dick
In the canteen there is rubbish all around
You could get lost and never be found
All the food makes my stomach crunch
I wish I was on packed lunch.

Adam Sturgeon (13)
Hurworth Maths & Computing College

Night-Time!

In the cold, damp darkness of the starry night,
I watch the houses fall asleep,
I see a violent fight.
I see a man fall over,
Onto a path edge,
I see a stray dog called Rover,
Scamper into a hedge.
I see homeless people lying on the street,
Waiting with people with change to spare,
With a hat by their feet.
I can feel the coldness of the winter's air,
Nobody wants to know,
They don't care!

Clare Rudd (12)
Hurworth Maths & Computing College

Autumn Is Here

The wind is howling
It's cold outside
The mornings are misty and damp
The winds get stronger throughout the day
While the leaves pile high at the side of the road
In every shade of brown
They rustle and crack as we make our way home
And that says to me autumn is here.

Robyn Simpson (12)
Hurworth Maths & Computing College

My Mum

She isn't an angel
She hasn't got wings
She can't be a queen
Without diamond rings
She hasn't got everything
Money can buy
Some things she can't do
But she's willing to try
She's quick on her feet
And good with her hands
She knows all about me
And she understands
You'll know what I'll do
After looking around
I wouldn't swap my mum
For one million pounds!

Sophie Tedd (12)
Hurworth Maths & Computing College

My Puppy-Dog

My puppy-dog will never do,
The kinds of things I want him to,
I take him out and try my best,
When I go east, he runs west.

He often tiddles on the floor,
I wipe it up and he does one more,
But my puppy-dog thinks he knows what's best,
When I go east, he runs west.

Ashleigh Atkinson (12)
Hurworth Maths & Computing College

Friends

To talk to, to laugh
To cry and to cuddle
You need help when you're in a muddle
So turn to a friend
When you're feeling down
And they will turn your frown
The other way round.

Friends take you to town
And put away your frown
Because you're their friend
That's what they do
For a friend always loves you
They help you through the good times
And the bad
The best you can do is a brill favour back.

Jordan Atkinson (12)
Hurworth Maths & Computing College

The Peach

The peach! The peach!
Too far to reach!
To drop in my throat,
To eat remote!
I'd climb a wall,
But I'd only fall!
I'll throw a stone
Or break a bone
That's why I'm all alone!
Too far to climb
No peace can be mine
And I'm running out of time!
I'll throw a stone with all my strength
Oh my, it went quite a length!
Yes, it hit! It's coming down!
This news will echo around the town!
Celebrate! It's time to jive!
Oh gosh! It's alive!

Adam Wright (13)
Hurworth Maths & Computing College

The Storm

The rain poured
Children scrambled to safety
The rain poured
Ship swayed and rocked
The rain poured.

The waves crashed
Screams got louder
The waves crashed
Ship started sinking
The waves crashed.

Kathryn Parker (13)
Hurworth Maths & Computing College

Taking Family For Granted

Mothers, fathers, sisters, brothers,
Always here, today, yesterday,
Think that they are always here,
Until the time you can't see them for the rest of your days.

Thousands, millions of families,
Hate their brothers or sisters,
Taking them for granted,
Until the time when the tears drop for sorrow and forgiveness.

One day they are here,
One day they are not,
That day when you have lost them,
You will cry and have the incurable wound in your heart.

Youssef Mahmoud (14)
Hurworth Maths & Computing College

The Snail

The big snail
He cries and wails
As he makes his trail
The winter is here
What snails always fear
As it is too cold for them to hear
There is no food
Which puts them in a mood
Therefore he isn't a cool dude
Time is passing on
Where he is the only one
Because he can't find anyone
The lonely big snail
Goes into hiding in a pail.

Emma Brentley (12)
Hurworth Maths & Computing College

The Storm

The waves were crashing
Crashing against the boat
Everyone was crying
Crying for help
Help that no one gave us

The cries for help
The cries for help
Help which no one gave us.

Leah Foley (13)
Hurworth Maths & Computing College

Nothing

Bombs banging, people scared.
Guns shooting, people hurting.
People screaming, people scared.
Why all the pain? For what . . .
Nothing, nothing at all.

Katherine Hobson (13)
Hurworth Maths & Computing College

Autumn

The autumn leaves are falling
Tumbling to the ground
Falling so gently, not making a sound
Piles of colours, yellow, orange and brown
A colourful carpet covering the ground.

The trees now look bare
And the birds have all flown
Migrating to a much warmer home
How sad the trees look not having a single leaf.

Jamie Myers (12)
Hurworth Maths & Computing College

Life!

There are ups and downs in life
And sometimes you can go as high as kites
But just remember if you come down
To always land with two feet on the ground.

When you're happy always show it
Because this world needs a bit of courage
And when you're down
Just put on a smile
Because the kid next to you might be in a happy style.

But no matter where you are in life
Always smile
Because after all
Everybody needs to be in a happy style.

Beth Frankland (12)
Hurworth Maths & Computing College

Autumn

The leaves are falling from the trees,
Most of the trees have no leaves,
Red, orange, yellow and brown,
A heavy rustle blows the leaves down.

Autumn time has come at last,
It will be just like it was in the past,
The leaves come down very fast,
Especially when the wind blows one big blast.

Autumn time has come at last.

Megan Hall (13)
Hurworth Maths & Computing College

Winter

Winter is cold
Want to go out
Lots of things to talk about

Winter is cold
Winter is bitter
The frost on the trees shines like glitter

Winter is cold
Winter is freezing
I have a cold and can't stop sneezing

Winter is cold
The snow is so deep
It's blowing a gale, I can't sleep.

Winter is cold
There is a storm
I go downstairs and wrap up warm.

Winter is cold
It's a terrible thing
But I look forward
To next year's spring.

Ben Harper (12)
Hurworth Maths & Computing College

Frog

A frog is a lumpy creature,
That jumps around all day,
He swims about in the water,
And he just popped up to say,
Ribbit!

Vicky Moffatt (13)
Hurworth Maths & Computing College

The Playground
(On a 'normal' day)

I stand alone in the playground . . .
Looking.
Looking at all the people
Laughing and poking fun, and usually a punch or two,
It's 'normal'.

One of them walks past me . . .
Staring.
Staring as if I'm from another planet,
'Three pounds fifty at Harry's on a night get an air cot,'
It's 'normal'.

My friend comes, says hi . . .
Talking.
Talking, though we already know the conversation,
Same old rubbishy jokes, same clichéd words exchanged.
It's 'normal'.

The rusty old bell rings . . .
Droning.
Droning as if we can't hear it
Off to the same stinky lessons we have past heard of,
It's 'normal'.

What's normal?
Normal.
Free from any mental illness; sane,
Relating to or characterised by average intelligence or development,
Fitting in with everyone else.

Do you really want to be the same as everyone else?
I mean . . . why?
You be you and I'll be me.
Why not just break the rules for a change?
I don't want to be anyone else!

Paul Dees (13)
Hurworth Maths & Computing College

My True Friend

There he sat,
A vision in my head,
An oasis in the desert,
The teddy on my bed.

He sits there all day,
A 'treasure' my mum said,
A cloud with silver lining,
The teddy on my bed.

My teddy is my pride and joy,
He comforts me when I'm down,
I'd never give my true friend up,
My teddy should get a crown.

Laura Bennett (13)
Hurworth Maths & Computing College

Heaven

In Heaven there are shopping malls
to shop in every day,
there's no need for money
'cause in Heaven you don't pay.

The angels have experience,
they're *really, really* loud,
but they don't wear big white cloaks
or float around on clouds.

If Heaven was a place on Earth
I'd go there every day,
for shopping with my mates,
and partying all the way!

Alix Leach (14)
Hurworth Maths & Computing College

Just An Old Woman

Just an old woman
Sitting in her chair with a blank stare
The paths carved in her face are endless
She is unaware of time that passes and
Awaits nothing

She tunes her attention to the outside
The birdbath from her house
The autumn leaves and frosted grass
A sparrow flits to the ground
She loved birds once

Memories paint pictures in her head
A child on the floor, a red dress and laughter
Awareness and knowing light her eyes
Her beautiful eyes

Her hand moves for the arm of her chair
A brittle, speckled hand
She bends forward and gets up
Groaning slightly as her bones crack

A breeze billows her skirt and moves
Her wispy hair slightly
She moves to the bed and lies down
And closes her eyes

She never woke up the next morning
She was ready, willing and for once
They found a smile on her lips
Just an old woman.

Rohanna Aston (13)
Hurworth Maths & Computing College

The Night

A black blanket covers the day,
Twinkling lights reveal a star.
The moon keeps watch of all the land,
Owls sound their eerie hoot.
Badgers, foxes rummaging around,
The night gets chilly.
A mole pops its head up from the ground,
The tree boughs sway in the gentle breeze.
Some mice scurry away from the predators above.
The cat's beady eyes glisten in the darkness,
Bats flutter past the rooftops.
But the night seems silent.
The sun arises,
The day is starting,
And the night is dead.

Emma Walton (13)
Hurworth Maths & Computing College

Hallowe'en

It's Hallowe'en,
Witches fly around the sky,
Cackle and scream as they go,
In the distance, cats' eyes flicker,
Bats hang and fly,
Owls hoot and stare with eerie eyes,
Full moon shines as wolves howl and bark,
Children running, shouting,
'Trick or treat?'
So now you know the real Hallowe'en,
Scary isn't it!

Katie Bearpark (13)
Hurworth Maths & Computing College

Friends

F riends are
R eally
I ntelligent, they're never
E nvious of you,
N early all the time they're fun to be with,
D eserving the 'best friend' award, even though
S ometimes friends are moody and unkind,
    but they always make it up to you.

Rebekah Brydon (14)
Hurworth Maths & Computing College

The Lights Of A Boy Racer

Lights in the night
Frantically smear your face
Under the hood of fright
You have got to pace

Wheels are burning
To light the streets
For pure class turning
I got people to meet

Turbo-charged engines
Ground rumbling
No time for pensions
Sound booming

Tricked-up car
Live or die
Burn the tar
You've said bye!

James Walton (13)
Hurworth Maths & Computing College

The Greatest Team

N ew season kicks off today,
E very fan is shouting, 'Hooray.'
W e come to win the league again,
C an we get off to a flying start?
A ll our greatest are here today,
S hearer, Jenas, Dyer
T itus, Lee, Johnothan
'L ook lads, we need these games.'
E lland Road isn't easy place to come to.

U nder the pressure of Milner
N ewcastle win 1-0
I t's a great game
T he Riverside, the deciding game
E very fan is shouting, 'Hooray.'
D o we win the league today?

F resh smell and the title coming our way
O ur opposition in 2nd place
O ur captains shake
T he game kicks off
B oro open the scoring
A terrific goal Juninio
L et's bring the score back lads
L ee passes to Shearer, it's in the net, 1-1.

C oncluding minutes, still 1-1
L ads were on the break
U p the field, in the box
B ellamy, the winning goal!

Robbie Gardner (13)
Hurworth Maths & Computing College

Darlo Till I Die

New tricks to learn,
New skills to try,
I'll always say,
I'm Darlo till I die.

When times are hard,
I'll still stand by,
And I'll always say,
I'm Darlo till I die.

If we're relegated,
I know I'll be frustrated,
Still I'll always say,
I'm Darlo till I die.

Oliver Chapman (13)
Hurworth Maths & Computing College

Charlotta's Tale

She sits in her chair of grief,
Antique wood seeming like bitter fire,
Burning away her self-esteem,
Inside - mind empty, heart so brief.

If anything could create doom,
This battle had been lost,
Storms that once seemed worst,
Hold nothing to her tomb.

Her joyful past is now unknown,
From stories never told,
Charlotta's tale is a never-ending death,
Like patchwork graves unsewn.

Amy Ralph (13)
Hurworth Maths & Computing College

The Boro

Match day is upon us now
It's the Boro faithful that keep us proud
Day upon day, night upon night
Draw, win or lose, they still don't care
Leicester, Man U, Liverpool
Everyone's here to support us now
Shouting us on, game after game
Boro will always be the same
Riverside is buzzing today
Our top players are all here to stay
Ugo, Gaizka, Massimo
Gareth, Szilard, Juninho
Here they can always stand tall.

Finally the game kicks off
Our rivals Newcastle stand against us
Our defences have broken, 1-0 to them
Terrible start we must come back
Ball is in the net 1-1
A majestic header from Ugo, 2-1
Looks like we are going to win
Lots of pressure we withstand.

Could this be the victory we deserve?
Louder are the fans
Ultimately this is the only game that matters
Boro have won this excellent victory.

Matthew Phillips (13)
Hurworth Maths & Computing College

The Spheres

Mercury the messenger,
The lightest on his feet,
If you try to race him,
I'm sure you'll be beat.

Jewel of the heavens,
Venus, goddess of love,
Beautiful as a flower,
Gentle as a dove.

Mars, ever up for fighting,
Behold his fearsome lance,
Enemies flee before him,
At a single glance.

Jupiter, oh mighty king,
Ruler of them all,
Beware his deadly thunderbolt,
For on you it may fall.

Saturn, father of the king,
He taught them all he knew,
Of those mightier than him,
There are very few.

Uranus, he's the wisest,
Grandsire to the king,
Even though he's the oldest,
He still knows a thing.

Neptune, god of the waves,
The deep and all that's in it,
His mighty trident stirs the sea,
To a tempest in a minute.

Pluto inhabits the underworld,
God of those passed on,
The second you breathe your last,
To meet him you'll be gone.

Chris Barron (13)
Hurworth Maths & Computing College

Night

I am terrified of the night,
I'm only happy when it's light,
I'm not lying, this is true,
My reason I'm about to tell you.

Gremlins living under the bed,
A werewolf shaking its hairy head,
The floorboards rattle and the winds howl,
The monsters' stench is really foul.

A vampire's hands are covered in blood,
Nothing about tonight is good,
During the day I feel happy and bright,
But that feeling of dread comes back at night . . .

Rachel Metcalfe (12)
Hurworth Maths & Computing College

Storm

Blue is for the coldness of the sea mist spraying your face.
Red resembles the bloody pain of your sheer heartache,
Whilst black is for confusion and your mind is too awake.

The motion of the boat is identical to the swaying of my stomach.

The waves crashing,
The boat swaying,
The screams screaming.

Leading to one thought,
The thought of *death*.

Louise Foley (13)
Hurworth Maths & Computing College

Cats And Dogs

Cats and dogs are all the same,
They can see what is happening all around them.
They show no fear for what they hear,
But they can be scared deep down inside.
When they're lost, they are terrified for no one can see it.
I feel sad when they're lost.
It's sad to see a lost poster.
I hope you feel what I feel,
But to know what I know,
To show what I show,
To help the lonely cats and dogs.

Lauren Hume (13)
Hurworth Maths & Computing College

War

It is very serious
The atmosphere is terrifying.
It isn't a laugh,
They are walking along a death path.

For their country they will die,
Over their heads the enemy will fly.
They travel in thousands wherever they're sent,
When they arrive they will stay in a tent.

Years and years they go on for,
The death tally is going up more and more.
Children are asked to fight in them,
They turn from 'kids' into men.

As it comes to an end,
The victims are on the mend.
Seems like it went on forever,
People wish that it was a never.

Adam Hassan (13)
Hurworth Maths & Computing College

Hallowe'en

Ghosts and ghouls,
Haunt our schools,
At midnight,
They come to fight.

Monsters and witches,
Flicking the light switches,
In our bedrooms,
Are we all doomed?

Zombies of the dead,
Hunt for our heads,
Using them as lights,
Guiding them through the night.

Bats are squeaking,
Vampires peeking,
Wanting fresh blood,
If only they could.

Skeletons clanging,
Doors banging,
They all shout,
As they jump about.

Demons and devils,
Teach young rebels,
The tricks they do,
Could kill me and you!

So all these creatures,
Come out of the deep,
All have odd features,
To give you the creeps!
Hallowe'en is a time of fear,
Argh! Watch out! He's got a spear!

Gemma Arnold (13)
Hurworth Maths & Computing College

Animals

Man's best friend,
There till the end,
Cuddly and cute,
The loyal and comforting dog.

Independent yet friendly,
She comes stalking by,
With her nine lives intact,
The sure-footed cat.

The swallow flies free as the wind,
Happy to fly many miles,
Darting around,
So quick and so shy.

The enemy of farmers,
That lives anywhere,
From hedgerows to rubbish dumps,
The sly yet harmless fox.

Stacey Hodgson (13)
Hurworth Maths & Computing College

Horses

As wild as the wind
As free as the wind
Galloping
Galloping out across the plains
The thundering of their hooves
The tremble of the ground
The swishing sound of manes and tails
Flapping as they catch the wind
They are the spirits of the land
Galloping
Galloping freely as they go . . .

Jennifer Mitchell (12)
Hurworth Maths & Computing College

GCSE Coursework

G is for the genuine hard work that is to achieve my aim.
C is for commitment that I need to achieve my grade.
S is for the several hours of work that is needed to finish the course.
E is for effort that I need to put in to reach my goal.

C is for the continuous work I have to put in.
O is for the obscene amounts that I have to do.
U is for the useful after school classes that help me
  with my coursework.
R is for the ridiculous time I have to spend on my work.
S is for the several subjects that I have coursework for.
E is for the endless days at school.
W is for my worries of getting my coursework in on time.
O is for the outrageous tasks that they set me.
R is for rest, which I get very little of.
K is for knowledge that I need to do my coursework.

Clare Peacock (15)
Hurworth Maths & Computing College

A Shadow Passing Through

I try not to have these feelings
but I do
I need so much healing
for these open wounds.

I know your love for me isn't true
you don't feel the way for me
the way I do for you.

I shouldn't have let it get this far
eventually I will heal
but I'll be bound with the scars
from a love that wasn't real.

I will always have to hide
the way I feel inside
I mean nothing to you
just a shadow passing through.

Claire Todd (15)
Hurworth Maths & Computing College

Utopia?

To see a world in a grain of sand
A heaven in a wild flower
Hold infinity in the palm of your hand
And eternity in an hour.

Rekindle given love
Palm the nightly stars as they glisten
Secure peace from a dove
Capture the silence as you carefully listen.

Create your utmost desires
Tongue the languages sweet and splendour
See the ocean world as a torching fire
Cherish those words that you render.

Hold the bouquet close and capture the emanation
Gaze at the waters scintillating
Your life is now a compilation
Nature is at your waiting.

Find serenity in your muse
Blemish in the sun's kindness
Treasure those feelings you must not lose
Open your eyes, prevent blindness.

Compose your own rhythm
See the pure moonlight . . . so beautiful
Or forever be held in a prison
The snowflakes rest, they are so neutral.

Voices awake, you will shake
And all this ice will break
Confide in others and be like brothers
As you endure this utopia.

Romeela Rana-Rahman (15)
Hurworth Maths & Computing College

Perfection

I've been searching all my life for perfection,
Then I see it in his pasty complexion,
When I am sad he makes me cheerful,
After my teachers give me an earful.
When he's around I can never frown,
He turns my frown upside down.
How I wish for his embrace,
It would put a smile on my face.
When he's around I can hardly breathe,
My heart speeds up to a very fast speed.
My one wish is to be with him,
For all my life to eternity.

Laura Dillon (15)
Hurworth Maths & Computing College

The Storm

I was on a ship,
then everything started to flip,
we were in a storm,
while I was in my dorm.

The waves were crashing,
my head was bashing,
the sails were ripped,
the ship's paint was stripped.

Passengers were screaming,
crew was steaming,
we had to evacuate,
where is my mate?

Help me now,
to my god I made a vow,
to let us live,
me and Viv.

Rebecca Boyd (13)
Hurworth Maths & Computing College

The Storm

On a cruise ship there I was,
Sitting peacefully under the sun,
Then all of a sudden there came a crash,
And waves were hitting with a bash.
The sun had gone,
It went all dark,
Then a storm began to start.
The ship was swaying from side to side,
People running to save their lives.
The ship was sinking,
People were terrified.
The lifeboats had gone,
And we were all stranded
With nowhere to go.
We sank with the ship.

Kirsty Williamson (13)
Hurworth Maths & Computing College

The Storm

It was the beginning of a sail
People not thinking of a tale
The winds are blowing frantically loud
The lightning behind the dark gloomy cloud
The waves are rising over shore
Worse than ever seen before
Tears appear, lots of vomit
Hopefully the storm shall drop it
Back to my shaky and warm dorm
This is the world's most terrible storm.

Shaun Marshall (13)
Hurworth Maths & Computing College

Royal Cruise

On my royal cruise
I was having an afternoon snooze
When I awoke to a storm
I crept from my dorm
As the waves roared and rolled
The sails twirled and whirled
Then in came through the door
The broken mast fell to the floor
People screeched more and more
As the ship was broken through its core
The waves battered the remaining wreck
People desperately fled the deck.

Jessica Harris (13)
Hurworth Maths & Computing College

The Storm

The waves began furiously crashing
The chairs starting taking flight
Children were frantically screaming
Then day turned to night.

I was feeling worse for wear
People were sick everywhere
People running up and down
I took to the ground.

I couldn't sleep a wink
All I could hear was *crash, crash, crash*,
Then all was silent and still
It was all over.

Clare Holme (13)
Hurworth Maths & Computing College

The Storm

Children wanting sympathy
Their things were all aboard
The storm came crashing down
The sail twirled and whirled

> The water came spilling in
> The storm rained down
> The boat started tipping
> Down, down, down

We watched this from our little boats
There was nothing we could do
Down, down, down
Into the deep.

Lauren Mitchell (13)
Hurworth Maths & Computing College

Storm

The wind is powerful,
The rain is strong,
It won't be long
Until the lightning strikes,
The clouds are heavy, about to rain.

Then the rain pours down,
Smacking on the floor,
You could hear it behind the door.

The thunder is loud,
Loud as a drum.

Daniel Sutcliffe (13)
Hurworth Maths & Computing College

The Journey In The Longboat

Waves crashing
Wind howling
Rain charging
Boat rocking
Ship sinking
That's what I saw

        Adults panicking
        Children screaming
        Babies wailing
        OAPs weeping
        That's what I heard.

Coldness creeping
Tears prickling
Wind tickling
Eyes stinging
Feet numbing
That's what I felt.

        The ice from the cold
        The bitterness of the sea salt
        The unflavoured charging rain
        The sharpness of the pain
        The tingling of my dinner
        That's what I tasted.

The strongness of vomit
The never-ending seaweed
The untouchable sea salt
The overpowering scent of blood
That's what I smelt.

        Too strong
        Too wild
        Too painful
        Too powerful
        Too wet
        Was what was inside me.

The journey went on
The pain carried on
The strong wind surged
Then gradually . . .
All was still!

Neneh Kaur Binning (13)
Hurworth Maths & Computing College

The Storm

The sun was shining,
Whilst people were dining,
In the large wooden hall,
Then suddenly things started to fall.

A storm has hit,
And not just a bit.
It crashed on the sail,
Till the ship was so frail.

The lifeboats afloat,
So hop in a boat,
To get away from this,
So we can row to a place of bliss.

The ship went down,
We started to frown.
It twisted and cracked,
It sunk and snapped.

Look here, there's sand,
We've finally found land.
Everyone was free,
Everyone and me.

Chris Lapping (13)
Hurworth Maths & Computing College

Storm

There I lay,
Rocking and shaking,
Feeling terrified and started to pray,
I was staring into space, just dazing,
I was feeling sick,
I needed to go home,
This journey was taking the mick.

We were told to go, in a nice way though,
We jumped on the ship,
And set sail for this trip.
I went to my cabin later in the day,
Then I was disturbed by crashing noises,
I opened the door and had a look,
I stood, then fell down,
I would get up but I couldn't move,
I shouted for help,
People ran at my yelp.

Pav Toor (13)
Hurworth Maths & Computing College

School

Most of our childhood is spent at school,
We never have any time to play.
I feel like such a big fool,
Going to school every day,
Doing our work, and never getting time alone.
And what about that awful food,
24/7 I'll always moan,
I'm always in such a big mood.
I just don't get the point of school.
I feel like such a big fool.

Clare Eddy (12)
Hurworth Maths & Computing College

Shipwrecked

What was peaceful, quiet and calm,
Where the waves were rolling,
And the white horses once jumped,
For some 3 hours or less,
Was a death bowl for me and the rest.

It was on one Saturday morn,
The masts were snapped and the sails torn,
The waves rolled over the edge of the deck
The wrath of the sea was upon us.
I felt the wind pounding on my face,
And heard the desperate screams of my comrades
Echo throughout the fog-filled sky.

The lifeboats were launched into the fiery abyss,
But all to no avail.
1, 2, 3 or more were all ripped to shreds,
A lightning bolt shot down from the sky,
Plunging into the deck,
The boat began to split in two,
The waves were lashing the hull.
We heard a call, 'Abandon ship!'
But no one else could hear it.
They were all there on the face of the deck,
Staring into the sky.

Jack Dell (13)
Hurworth Maths & Computing College

The Storm

As we got into the lifeboat,
What a joy it was to see men in yellow coats,
Everything seemed calm,
The waves seemed smaller.

I could see no more,
The salt was in my eyes,
Gone were the strong seas,
As we sailed away I could sense happiness once again.

I looked back,
I could see the ship we once sailed,
Then it disappeared forever,
Down to the bottom it went.

As we entered the shore,
I could see my family,
And faces of people I knew,
What a wonderful feeling as my feet touched the ground.

Robert Edwards (13)
Hurworth Maths & Computing College

I Love You

I love you in the morning
I love you in the night
and when I see you standing
I hold my hand so tight
when I close my eyes
the world around me stops
how I feel my hand so soft
I love you lots and lots.

Gemma Baker (12)
Hurworth Maths & Computing College

War

Sirens are everywhere,
I just can't bear,
I stayed up all night,
Thinking about the fight,
The smell of blood,
Isn't at all good,
Soldiers always dying,
Everyone always crying,
Gunshots fly through my ears,
All I can feel are tears,
Morning is nowhere near,
The sky is so clear,
Creeping along the floor,
Reaching for the door,
I wanted to wake my mum,
The war had only just begun!

Nichola Bateman (12)
Hurworth Maths & Computing College

Brothers

Why do we have brothers?
They just really are *bad*.
They hide under the covers,
When my mum is mad.

Why do we have brothers?
They just get on your nerves.
They go out and play with others,
They are just a big curse.

Why do we have brothers?
I don't really know.
We love them like our mother,
But we don't really show!

Nathaniel Merriott (12)
Hurworth Maths & Computing College

My Brother

My brother is a pain sometimes,
But sometimes he's alright.
When he doesn't get his way,
He moans almost all day and night.

He's very good at football,
He plays on the left.
He runs very fast,
He scores with no deflect.

We have a game of Nightfire,
Where we destroy the phoenix base.
He likes watching The Simpsons,
He laughs out loud and pulls a funny face.

I wouldn't change him for another,
Because he is my brother.

Daniel Gayles (12)
Hurworth Maths & Computing College

My Friends

My friends are really important to me,
It's not as easy as if they grew on a tree!

There's my friend Stephanie who is a laugh,
And she has a dog called Saph!

Next there's Abby who is round the bend,
I'm so lucky she's my friend!

Then there's Liza who's really hyper,
She dances round like the Pied Piper!

Of course there's Tori whose stuff I lend,
But she's my bestest ever friend!

All in all I love my mates,
We are all into the same things not like Gareth Gates!

Paris Lowcock (12)
Hurworth Maths & Computing College

My Life

My parents are Martians
They come from Mars
When they were there
They could fit in a jar

I'm not sure what my brother is
But he's really weird
Maybe he's an alien
Or just a Tasmanian

Then there's my dog
She's the most human of us all
Even though she comes back
Just for a ball

I think my friends are human
Except their personality
I don't even care
About their popularity.

Stephanie Leonard (12)
Hurworth Maths & Computing College

SAS

They are sneaky, they are fast
They have done great things in the past
If you see them you better beware
Because you will be under their snare

They go undercover and set up an O P
They are so far in enemy territory they can't afford to be dopey
They always have a fall-back den
And nearly come back with all their men

They come home to no applause
For the heroics they have performed
They seem to disappear rather like a mist
But do they really exist
Mac's men?

Matthew Smith (12)
Hurworth Maths & Computing College

My Dog Jess

My dog Jess,
She's simply the best!

She is full of energy,
Which will never leave,
And is always there to play.

My dog Jess,
She's simply the best!

She loves her walks,
And likes being groomed,
But to sit and relax is never her favourite.

My dog Jess,
She's simply the best!

She never leaves my side,
When I am with her all the time,
And shows how loyal she is.

My dog Jess,
She's simply the best!

If she had the choice she would eat, eat, eat,
But never would she leave me alone,
Unless she was asleep.

My dog Jess,
She's simply the best!

Catherine Brown (13)
Hurworth Maths & Computing College

Match!

The match has started,
1 . . . 2 . . . 3 . . .
The opposition is scared of me
Step over left, step over right
At last I'm in the spotlight
'Pass, pass,' my teammates call
'I'm not passing, I'm keeping the ball!'
Bang . . . top corner, it's a goal!

Jonathan Weeks (12)
Hurworth Maths & Computing College

My Best Friends

My best friends, I know they care,
Because my best friends are always there.
I treat my friends like they treat me,
Because I know they want to be treated like they do treat me.

My best friends, I know they care,
Because my best friends are always there.
When I'm feeling down,
They make me happy, that's why I'd give them a crown.

My best friends, I know they care,
Because my best friends are always there.
They never leave me all alone,
And listen to the stories which I make up on my own.

My best friends, I know they care,
Because my best friends are always there.
Let's face it,
They won't fake it,
They are the best,
Better than the rest.

Sabriye Wallis (12)
Hurworth Maths & Computing College

Football Crazy

The match has started
According to the referee
Barry Conlen is on the ball
Not listening to the teammates as they call
He skins them down the left
He skins them down the right
His shot strikes the net like a piece of dynamite.

Craig Peacock (12)
Hurworth Maths & Computing College

Harry

I have a pony named Harry,
He's full of mischief and fun,
I have a pony named Harry,
I treat him as my son,
I have a pony named Harry,
I ride him all the time,
I have a pony named Harry,
He's normally committing a crime,
I have a pony named Harry,
He's really very sweet,
I have a pony named Harry,
He sometimes stands on my feet,
I have a pony called Harry,
No matter what he does,
He is still my favourite pony,
With his kisses and his hugs.

Becky Mullett (12)
Hurworth Maths & Computing College

My Dog Called Ben

My dog Ben,
He's half the age of ten,
He runs around,
And then sits down,
That's my dog called Ben.

My dog Ben,
He goes to sleep and then,
He wakes up to play,
And then he doesn't stop all day,
That's my dog called Ben.

My dog Ben,
He likes to go in my den,
He sniffs around,
Without a sound,
That's my dog called Ben.

My dog Ben,
He's gone to bed, and when,
He gets up there isn't a peep,
Because he's gone to sleep,
That's my dog called Ben!

Francesca Heath (12)
Hurworth Maths & Computing College

Football

F ootball is fantastic
O verall it's the best
O ver and above the rest
T oon army are my favourite
B all, you couldn't have the game without it,
A drenaline, the rush you get when your team score
L isten to the crowd roar
L ove footie for evermore.

David Robbins (11)
Lord Lawson of Beamish School

Britain

Britain is hot,
Britain is cold,
Britain's weather can never be told.

Down in the streets of London,
Big Ben stands,
Can you hear the brass bands?

The Millennium Bridge,
Stands with pride,
It tilts for boats when people go on rides.

Go to the seaside,
In the west,
You will see it's the best.

However on the beach in the east,
See the donkeys gallop by,
It's time for me to go *bye-bye!*

Victoria Routledge (11)
Lord Lawson of Beamish School

When Henry Ruled The Kingdom

When Henry VIII ruled this kingdom
The land was fresh and green
He ruled it with all his wives
And always needed a new queen

He spent his money on himself
The land was left to rot
When he died in agony
His memory was never forgot

The man was ill and lay in bed
His wife became nursemaid
He died in peace knowing he had a son
To carry on his workload.

James Welsh (11)
Lord Lawson of Beamish School

Britain

B ritain is one of the smallest countries in Europe,
R eminds me of a dot,
I t's got one of the best football teams in
T he world has Britain, and they're called Newcastle United,
A nd it's got a very good capital city called London.
I like Britain.
N ow I might not be a very good poem writer, but I tried.

Billy Harwood (11)
Lord Lawson of Beamish School

Seaside

S ea lapping up against the sand
E ars listening to the sound of the sea
A lbatross
S oaring high
I n the sky
D igging the sand
E ating ice cream in the sun.

Ben Taylor (11)
Lord Lawson of Beamish School

Britain

B est fish and chips you will ever have
R ainy always, sun at times
I n the city, Big Ben chimes
T ony Blair is losing hair
A t each time children go to school
I n the Tyne rubbish flows
N obody good, nobody bad, but we all live in Britain.

David Talbot (12)
Lord Lawson of Beamish School

The Best Of Great Britain

Great red buses driving by
Red, small or tall
Engines ticking like a clock
Angel of the North is such a sight
The Millennium Bridge standing with might

Buckingham Palace is where the Queen lives
Ringing in my ears are Big Ben's chimes
In Piccadilly Circus, people come in droves
The sad disappearance of the Millennium Dome
A group of Japanese tourists snappy with their cameras

In their finest jewellery and clothes, people visit the West End
No matter where I roam, Great Britain is my home.

Nicole Sharkey (11)
Lord Lawson of Beamish School

Britain

An extraordinary country
Living peacefully in houses

From Newcastle to Plymouth
England grows strong

It is the great inventor of football, rugby and cricket
A small country brings so much joy

Royalty, the Prime Minister and even the army
Giving us protection but receiving nothing

But it's not that bad
For we receive the trust of Britain

So now, each day when I think of Britain
I will think of inventors, towns and even safety
But most of all what an extraordinary country.

Alex Bills (11)
Lord Lawson of Beamish School

Changing Weather

Winds that bring the icy snow.
I wonder where the hedgehogs go?
It never gets any warmer than cool.
Do fish get frostbite in the pool?
Yet when the sun comes out bright,
The buds start to bloom in the sun's warming light.
The cold gets warmer bit by bit.
It's funny how daffodils recognise it.
Summer's here with long, warm days.
Do bees smell pollen in its warming rays?
As days shorten and nights cut in,
You wonder what the autumn will bring!
Gloves and scarves and woolly hats.
Carpets made for home-loving cats.
Darkness rules the land once more,
Turn on the heating and close that door!

Laura Charlton (11)
Lord Lawson of Beamish School

Beautiful Britain

Beautiful Britain, how you gleam.
All your magnificent places shine so marvellously.
Bridges, buildings, rivers and streams.

Faces, faces, so many faces.
How you attract so many different faces.
Citizens of the world unite.

Rain, snow, sun and wind.
Weather is the topic of conversation.
Beautiful Britain, how you gleam.

Kyle Davie (11)
Lord Lawson of Beamish School

Typical Britain

B is for Blair, Tony Blair, prime minister of Great Britain
R is for Royal family who reign over Britain
I is for Isigonis the designer of the Great Britain classic, the Mini
T is for the Tower of London where the Queen keeps her jewels
A nd don't forget England, Scotland and Wales, the other three,
I is for Ireland, across the Irish sea.
N is for Newcastle, the greatest city in the north east.

Matthew Jennings (11)
Lord Lawson of Beamish School

My Poem

Patchwork fields
Hot Sunday meals
Castles and keeps
Mountains and peaks
Cold days out
Never a doubt
Rain and drizzle
The bacon goes sizzle
Churches and pews
Many nice views
White cliffs of Dover
Fields full of clover
Kings and queens
Lots of great scenes

England's our home
And this is my poem.

Lauren Turner (11)
Lord Lawson of Beamish School

Fish And Chips

F lying seagulls swooping around me,
I nside shops people gaze at the sea,
S and sparkles in the sun,
H oliday time has just begun.

A nglers catch their fish for tea,
N aughty children watch with glee,
D ogs are running on the sand.

C rabs scurrying onto land.
H olidaymakers eat their chips,
I rresistible to their lips,
P hotos taken, good time had,
S treets are empty, looking sad.

Paul Old (11)
Lord Lawson of Beamish School

World War II

Soldiers fight, soldiers die
They look down from the sky
Now they see both you and me enjoying ourselves in London.

Women waited, waiting to cry,
Thinking, *please, don't you die*
Where did you go?
Well I'll never know,
But when that place blew
I knew it was you
Taking part in World War II.

Abby Kelford (12)
Lord Lawson of Beamish School

Britain

Went to London, rode the Eye,
Right up there, it's so high,
Looked around, what's to be seen?
Straight ahead, oh! There's the Queen.
And look to the left, who's over there?
Well what do you know, it's Tony Blair.
To the right all Britain's power,
Ruled one time from the tower.
Wembley Stadium is even nearer,
Who's kicking the ball? It's Alan Shearer.
Further down the river is the Dome,
Big Ben rings, it's time to go home.

Liam Hall (11)
Lord Lawson of Beamish School

London

L ondon is cool, it's the place to be
O n top of the London Eye you will see the beautiful sea
N early everyone I know likes it there
D on't you know the Queen sits there in her chair?
O h go on, you have to go
N obody (on Earth) is going to say *no!*

Holly Nevin (11)
Lord Lawson of Beamish School

Britain

B ritain is where you eat fish and chips
R ides and funfairs
I ntelligent students at school
T oday is a special day
A t the beach, donkey rides are good
I n the swimming pool children play
N othing is more fun than *Britain*.

Danny Riley (11)
Lord Lawson of Beamish School

At The Beach

The donkeys walked along the beach
The sand was soft and warm
The children were waiting to have a ride
'50p a go,' he said
The sea was boiling hot
You could see the feeding buckets and the water for the donkeys
People were surfing in the sea
As the donkeys came back, the children started getting excited
The lifeguard was on watch
The children had their ice creams.

Christopher Tiffin (11)
Lord Lawson of Beamish School

This Is A Wonderful Place

The UK is a wonderful place
It does get sunny here just in case
You are wondering what happens here in the UK
Are you ready? Sit down now, it's OK
The wind and the sleet and of course the snow
It does not shine all the time, oh no, no, no
This is a wonderful place!
But then there is the good old sun
The joy and the happiness and also the fun
Come on everybody, do we love the warmth?
I hear a big scream, '*Yeah!*'
The fish and chips that we eat all day long
The shops and the food, oh we couldn't go wrong
Then all the leaves fall on the ground
Brown and all crusty
This is still a wonderful place!

Kayleigh Trainer (11)
Lord Lawson of Beamish School

Fish And Chips

Fresh from the sea
It's brought battered to me
Salt 'n' vinegar if you please
Have to say no to mushy peas
Nice 'n' tasty
Cod 'n' tatie
Have to have them, think they're great
In newspaper, no plate
Pick up with my fingers
Scranchions added, the taste just lingers.

Callum Russell (11)
Lord Lawson of Beamish School

The Bridge

A bridge is a giant on hands and knees,
Kneeling down to fill a gap,
Allowing people and cars to cross
Upon his back.

A bridge is a giant of stone or steel,
With a back so hard he doesn't feel,
The trouncing of tyres or the hammering of heels.

A bridge is a giant with legs astride,
Welcoming through from far and wide,
Graceful ships that slowly glide.

A bridge is a giant who carries the roads
And the trucks and lorries with heavy loads,
A giant who stays there night and day
And who never gets up and goes away.

Rachel Hodgson (12)
Moorside Community College

After A Shakespearean Sonnet (Of Sorts!)

The husky tones that rested in her voice
The way she seemed to melt away my time
Whenever I could see her I'd rejoice
That she had sworn to be forever mine
I stand upon the hill and hold her hand
For at the eye of the storm we're secure
Together we observe a dying land
She is the only thing of which I'm sure.
I know we'll be together till I die
Yet sometimes in the winter nights I think
I might not be the only one, and sigh
That thought's enough to drive me to the brink
I'm sure this is but my inner debate
I ask myself if now, I am too late.

Matthew Nash (15)
Moorside Community College

The BMW

The great BMW
Best car ever made.
Smooth, fast, classic
Like an arrow through the sky
Like a speedboat through the water
It makes me feel fast
Like a jet in the sky.
The great BMW
Reminds us how quickly we can go.

Jason Barsby (12)
Moorside Community College

But I Have To Stay Home

I wish to care
I wish to share
But I have to stay home.
I wish to eat tea
I wish to act like me
But I have to stay home.
I wish to have love
I wish to have life
But I wish for you to stop
Me having a fight
But I have to stay home.
I hope to be fair
I hope to brush my hair
But I have to stay home.
I wish to drive an expensive car
I wish to live in a star
But I have to stay home.
I wish to stay alive
But I don't wish to live in a beehive
But I have to stay home.

Lauren Dyer (12)
Moorside Community College

The Autumn

The greenest leaves turn golden-brown,
Reds and oranges all around.
The sun starts to rest its head,
Behind the trees on their leafy bed.
The nights get longer, longer, longer,
The winds get stronger, stronger, stronger.
The flowers they close and fall asleep,
And wait till spring when again they peep.
There are piles of leaves where there were none before,
But when the snow comes the autumn is no more.

Amber Cranson (12)
Moorside Community College

In The Spring

In the springtime March, April and May
The sheep were brought in and there they will stay.
They get bigger and bigger and bigger still
You must wait and wait and wait until
At first just one appears, a white, fluffy fleece
The sound of the lambs echoed by the geese.
You see the first one, then two, three and more
Like captured clouds above the seashore
Each one no different from the one before,
Playing together, they leap and bleat.

The spring turns to summer, the lambs to sheep
They are calm now and no longer bleat and leap.
The sun goes down it's getting late
Only to repeat at a later date.

Kaye Lowery (15)
Moorside Community College

The Lone Flag

I went to school as normal
Went to English, maths and art
Painted a picture of a flag.

I went home out on the TV
It looked like a good film
About an attack on the World Trade Centre.

There was a lone flag flying
Slowly it burned with a fierce fiery flame
Then a plane flew by and into the tower.

Then I realised that it wasn't a film
It was the real thing
The remote fell to the floor and broke

Just like many hearts in New York.

Richard Walford (15)
Moorside Community College

The Day To Remember

It was a day of sadness
it all happened so suddenly
a day to remember

Sound of cries from the other rooms
made me remember Charmaine
the little girl who was so special to me

The doctors and nurses running around
the answers to my questions
will never be found

The smell was so cold
and the lights so bright
when I looked away my eyes stung

She was only aged one and so sweet
the sound of her voice in my heart
began to repeat

When I got home I sat and cried
the thought of what happened
made me feel worse inside

As she lay at rest
I know she was in peace
I will always remember her small heartbeat.

Lynsey Davison (15)
Moorside Community College

The Bulky Tiger

The bulky tiger
Only years old
Large, powerful, fast
Like a shark bumping a boat
Like an elephant jumping
I feel fear, I feel love
My blood feels like ice and fire
The bulky tiger.

Gilly Nelson (13)
Moorside Community College

The Good Times

Life, when I was young was great
I hadn't a care in the world.
Everything I did was great
From climbing trees
To twitching knees
Yes life, when I was young, was great.

Teenage life is hard.
It's even harder when you're alone;
Girls become part of your life
Smoking and drinking too.
Making decisions is hard
The life I had has gone.
No more climbing trees
Or twitching knees.

Being young was great
But I'm older now
All I do is get into trouble
And on my face signs of stubble.

Shaun Connolly (15)
Moorside Community College

The Polar Bear

The polar bear,
As white as snow.
Cold, fluffy, loveable
A shimmering diamond.
Like a ball of snow,
Lonely and cold
Like a small, homeless child.
The polar bear
Reminds us how lucky we are
To have warm, safe houses.

Kate Cranson (12)
Moorside Community College

Penny

I slouched all day at school
Watching the hours drag by
At four o'clock our school bus drove me home

In the living room my father
Was sitting in silence
A tear rolling down his face

My brother was in his bedroom
Music blasting out of his speakers
My mam was in the kitchen sobbing

I sat down slowly on the settee
And asked where my dog Penny was
My father looked at me and sobbed, 'She's gone!'

I remembered when I would
Play with my Penny in the garden
Watching her run after her ball

I shed a tear for every laugh, for every game we shared.

Lea Griffiths (15)
Moorside Community College

My Bedroom

My bedroom,
My very own room,
Magical, cosy, warm,
Like a fairy-tale palace,
Like every girl's dream.
It makes me feel happy,
Like a girl with all the diamonds in the world.
My bedroom,
My very own fairy tale.

Levi Taylor (12)
Moorside Community College

About Life

Just born, young and wild like
the trees blowing in the wind.
Parents' ambition and expectations
so so high.
Just in the eyes they glare and stare.

Laughter and joy when first born,
late and sleepless nights get them both uptight.

Getting older means parents' nightmare.
Selfish, silly and stupid your attitude goes wild.

Turn 13 teenager, drinking, drugs
may get involved to ruin your life in one big swoop.

Now I am here with neither of those,
life going good, so I'll be ready for the big bad world.

Paul Clarke (15)
Moorside Community College

The End Of An Era

The telephone rang
And I picked up the receiver.
On the other end I heard my mum crying.

She said, 'Your grandad has gone.'
I got a big knot in my throat.
I couldn't hold my tears back.
I began to cry.

The day wore on,
Later my auntie took me home.
I really wanted to see my grandad.

I walked into the living room
And saw a small pale white man.
My eyes started to fill up
I ran to my room.

An integral part of my life had gone forever.

Caroline Slater (15)
Moorside Community College

Which Ball To Use

In my hand lies the rubber-gripped club
It lies there as snug as a bug.
The football stories all year through
But I just want to keep on using that club.
Hitting the ball feels so good,
Swinging, smacking and seeing
The ball fly through the air like a bird.

I look back and hear those stories,
I know that my father wishes
For me to do as he's done, football.
He kicked that ball in the air as did my grandfather.
He would kick the ball in the back of the net,
Meanwhile, taking a large chunk of turf with it.

I know that he wants me to carry on the game
As he and my grandfather did.
But the ball does not rest on my foot
As it rests on my club.
The golf ball.

Andrew Lee (15)
Moorside Community College

The Grey Koala Bear

The grey koala bear
Sleeps nineteen hours a day.
Slow, sleepy, starving
Like a newborn baby
A mum's cub.
It makes me care
Like a mother cares for her child.
The grey koala bear
Reminds us who brought us
Into the world.

Katie Affleck (12)
Moorside Community College

Grandad

Today I woke to find you gone
This is the day my life has gone.
Someone so special, someone so kind
That someone is you, my grandad.
You've left me here
Without a word
Without a goodbye.

Hours and hours have gone by
Life now seems not worth going on.
I miss you loads
I love you loads
Please come back I need you loads.

Today I woke to find you gone
This is the day my life has gone.
I love you loads
Am missing you loads
But one day, I know we'll meet again.

Laura McGregor (15)
Moorside Community College

The Bully

Children stop their running and playing,
Teachers stop their teaching and working,
'But why?' was the cry,
'Why should I be the one to go?'
She felt like crying, she was feeling low.
The bully was laughing with her head tipped back,
'Now listen to me, I'm the best you brat.'
The teachers were walking over,
'Come with us now please Miss Clover.'
Her parents were waiting there, in the room,
'Come on darling you're moving school.'

Lauren Robinson (12)
Moorside Community College

Grandad

I love to hear your wild stories
Even if they are scary and gory.

I love how you battled the pirates in my dream
Or how you were the best player on the football team.

I love it when you fought the soldiers in WWII
Or when you tamed a tiger, which escaped from the zoo.

I love to hear that wonderful tale
When you got caught in the roar of the gale.

I love it when you used all your might
Or when you travelled faster than the speed of light.

I love to remember when you used to say
'I promise to take you one day.'

I hate to remember that you're not here
You were the only one, who caught my tear.

Caroline Wyatt (14)
Moorside Community College

My Cute Dog

My cute dog
Is only small.
White, furry, brave.
White like the snow
Furry like a bear.
Makes me happy
When he is near.
Makes me feel safe
Like I have a guard.
My cute dog
Reminds me of cuddly toys.

Emma Bramley (12)
Moorside Community College

Autumn

I love to see the sun set low in an autumn sky
As pink candyfloss clouds float silently by
I love the blissful joy of an early morning ramble
Where fine ribbons of mist shroud fern and thorny bramble
The first bite of frost glistens in the trees
I feel the chilled breath of autumn is present in the breeze
Leaves of honey, copper and burnished brown
Accompanied on their journey by seeds and thistledown
The heavy scent of fertile earth disturbed beneath my feet
As I bear witness to the haste of the summer's retreat
For the woodland's population all take the greatest care
In their fervent harvest of Mother Nature's fare
Autumn heralds not death but gentle sweet repose
And whispers a gentle lullaby as the eyes of summer close.

Rachel Drury (14)
Moorside Community College

The Moon

The shining moon
Hanging in space forever
Huge, round, bright
Like some cheese lighting the night.
Like a bright button on a black coat.
It makes me feel minute
Like a star fading as it gets light.
The shining moon
Reminds us how dull we are.

Marc Milburn (12)
Moorside Community College

Sail It!

I love to see the reservoir shining bright
And small boats sailing to the north.
I love to see the fish jumping high in the light
And ducks disappearing down below.
The ripples disperse round and slow
Where sails rustle and leaves crackle,
Where spacesuited men crouch in boats
And sail the water almost afloat.
I like the cool water spray splashing on my face
The bows plane gracefully through the water
I love the wind-made speed
My racing heart it does feed.
Another windy morning invites us to play
And wills our return to sail another day!

Alex Milburn (14)
Moorside Community College

The Moon

The bright moon,
Shining boldly at night.
Big, round and ablaze,
A big ball of cheese.
As big as the sun,
It makes me feel small,
As small as a grain of sand.
The bright moon
Reminds us size doesn't matter.

Helen Woodward (13)
Moorside Community College

Four Seasons

The summer has come
I wish it would stay
It won't be the same
It's going day by day.

Soon autumn will come,
For a while it will stay,
The trees lose their leaves,
They all blow away,

Just like the summer, the autumn will go,
We wake up one morning and we have snow.

Brrr, it's cold, now I wish winter would go,
Winter stays longer, time goes very slow.
The days get warmer the birds start to sing,
Hooray, now it's spring.

There are lambs in the field and farmers making hay.
I'm happy to say, at last summer's on its way.

Annette Simpson (12)
Moorside Community College

The Amazing Tiger

The amazing tiger
Out and free in the wild.
Huge, roaring, fierce
Like a flash of fire piercing the air
Like a bird, free as can be.
Makes me feel brave
Like the eyes of the tiger are my own.
The amazing tiger
Reminds us how brave we are
How strong it makes us feel.

Pearl-Susanne Davison (12)
Moorside Community College

A Dog

A dog is man's best friend
you wonder why that's said?
He'll protect you while you're sleeping,
lying at the bottom of your bed.
They come in different shapes and sizes
but yours is always the best,
because he's smarter, braver,
cuter and more loyal than all the rest.

Sarah Louise Bridgewater (14)
Moorside Community College

My Last Day At Barnardby School

9am open the door
just to run into school once more.
Run to class, am I late
or will I again be the bully's bait?
I am right, there he is waiting for me
and only because he thinks he's hard
he makes me run around the yard.
There he stands with his fist like steel
he shouts at me, 'To me, you kneel!'
'Kneel to you?'
'You will pay.'
I'm sure glad it's my last day.
One bad blow, one sprained wrist
Now it all just seems like mist.
One more blow and I'd have been dead
Buried into the earth's bed.
I am free from my life of hiding
I am free from all confiding.

Kimberley Walton (14)
Moorside Community College

Alone

Do you ever get the feeling you're completely alone?
The only voice you listen to is you,
In a room where everybody is yelling,
There's only one voice you hear,
Your own.

You could be standing at a bus stop
Headphones in your ears,
But it's all a ruse,
You never hear the song words
All you listen to is your own contemplation.
Your own.

In your own head you could be anyone;
A magician, a bit older,
There's no limit.
Everything you dream of being,
But that's all it is
A vision, a dream of the near future,
Your own.

Kimberley Stephenson (12)
Moorside Community College

The Hurricane

Wild, wild the hurricane, the wind blowing,
Destruction is its goal, everything ruining,
Don't stand in its way, or you'll be regretting,
Its savage intentions are extremely threatening,
Swoosh, swoosh the gales cry, whistling and inflicting,
It hunts its prey, chasing and attacking,
Its power is impressive, but its endurance is fading,
The nightmare is over, but will soon be returning.

Steven Livingstone (14)
Moorside Community College

The Leopard

He grips the earth with little sound,
Through the weeds his feet do bound,
Along to the place, where they are found.

The wrinkled sand blew to the east,
He sprang upon the struggling beast
And within moments, began to feast.

Steven Clarke (14)
Moorside Community College

The Wolf

He howls at the moon with an open jaw,
Standing proudly on the rocky floor,
Then to his land he will go.

Crawling along with an arched neck,
Like a sergeant he places his pack
And seizes upon his prey's back.

Lee Smith (14)
Moorside Community College

Dream Boy

I love to see you smile and laugh,
when you're walking down the winding path.

I love to see you at my door,
my heart beats faster, more and more.

When you kiss me on the cheek,
my knees go wobbly and quickly weak.

If only I knew but who you were,
you would not look so like a blur.

Oh boy of my dreams, so sweet,
you lift me high, off my feet.

Leanne Bullamore (14)
Moorside Community College

The Snake

The snake slithers along the ground
His body long, his head round
Moving stealthily without a sound.

He swallows the vole whole
Then slithers back to his hole
Enjoying his tasty vole.

David Stephenson (14)
Moorside Community College

The Snake

He slowly slithers across the rainforest floor,
Looking for victims by sensing lots more,
Soon he finds what he's been searching for,

Waiting to strike like a bat out of hell,
The target's heartbeat turns into a knell,
There's death in the air, the dreaded smell,

Like nothing's happened he slides away,
Trying really hard to digest his prey,
And quietly awaits his next killing day.

Rebecca Grant (14)
Moorside Community College

My Baby Bro

Whether he's singing or crawling,
Laughing or bawling,
Playing or talking,
He's still my brown-eyed baby bro learning.

Smiling or pouting,
Screaming or shouting,
Running or walking,
He's still my brown-eyed baby bro learning.

Jasmine Glasgow (14)
Moorside Community College

The Feline

Hunched down low in the garden, he's hiding
gradually advancing, he's slyly creeping
A mouse scuttles by so I guess he's hunting
in search of his prey, he is soundlessly prowling
Each paw step he captures it gets more frightening
like a tiger in the wild, every bit is exciting
I watch in awe as his furry lips he's licking
his bloodthirsty eyes in every direction are looking
The grass around him is gently whispering
as the wind rustles through, the suspense is chilling.
He arrests his feast. His result is satisfying.

Lauren Webster (14)
Moorside Community College

Different

I hate it when I get funny looks from people passing by,
It makes me stop and think, *why do I actually try?*
I try to look my best, but it's obviously not that good,
They cannot understand me, but I really wish they would.
I don't follow like sheep as others always do,
I dress in Gothic clothes and I know that it is true.
People always brand me and hardly talk to me.
It doesn't really affect me, 'Just watch and you will see,'
As they shout abuse, I laugh it off in my head,
Though sometimes, just sometimes, it makes me go all red.
They don't even know me, so why do they shout that stuff?
Sometimes I just want to shout, *'Right then, that's enough!'*

Kathryn Tyler (14)
Moorside Community College

The Snake

The snake slithers along the ground,
Silently hunting for its prey, until it's found,
It stalks the mouse without a sound.

The snake leaps to strike its prey,
But the victim manages to get away,
It slithers away, to return another day.

Gareth Ferguson (14)
Moorside Community College

My Comfy Bed

My comfy bed
Is in the corner of my room
Bouncy, warm, cosy
Like a cloud in the summer sky
Like my own private world
It makes me feel safe
Like I'm surrounded by 100 guards.
My comfy bed
Reminds me that everyone
Needs some sleep.

Danielle Albon (13)
Moorside Community College

Six-Week Holiday!

'School is out,'
We scream and shout,
Smiling faces are all about.

The happiness has just begun,
Everyone is in the sun,
Having lots of fun.

Gemma Lister (14)
Moorside Community College

The Lake District

A clouded mind,
Mist over thoughts,
Coats mountains,
Lakes, like mirrors, reflect images,
Good and bad.

Streams, like capillaries in life,
Only open when it rains,
Otherwise they are unimportant,
Join the sea, the heart.

A bare rock face,
Empty; wounds in the soul,
Exposed, sometimes cravassed,
Wrinkled with age,
Otherwise concealed,
A broken heart,
A broken soul.

The mountains so tall,
They close in on you,
Making you feel tiny,
Insignificant,
As an insect in the workings of the universe,
Filling you with reverence and awe.

Jessica Robb (14)
Polam Hall School

He

The silent stillness of the suave black night,
For the world slept in irresistible slumber,
Only He remained awake,
Through the drowsy town, He lumbered.

The ash leaves rippled in the cool night's breath,
And the moon cast its tranquillising light,
But He plodded onwards, each step sapped his strength,
Whilst his surroundings embraced the night.

The diamonds tossed amongst the clouds
Sparkled down upon this peace,
But never once did He look up,
His pain was starting to increase.

The black sheet that was thrust over the world,
When the sun decided to descend,
Could not blanket him from his agony,
This was torture - it had no end.

His pain was excruciating, He could not go on,
He battled to stumble one small pace,
He trudged into an alleyway, to die a private death,
In this secluded dingy place.

The owls hollered howls of mournful song,
And it rained the tears of the night,
He sank to the ground, He could not go on,
This was the end of his fight.

As the first rays of light peered over the town,
He began to weep,
The day stole the darkness, when the world awoke,
But He began his eternal sleep.

The sun will rise, the sun will set,
But He will not awaken,
Our world is so harsh, only the night will see,
His life should not have been taken.

Suzie Millar (11)
Polam Hall School

Dark Snow

Smoky, white powder,
Swirling around,
On a throbbing wind,
Silent.

Muted by snow,
Muffled by clouds,
A thick, opaque white
Closes in.

A white hole
Of light, in layers
Of tracing paper clouds.
All bright,

Yet in shades of
Blue, frosty light,
Colours dusted
In a grey hue.

A place in hibernation,
Quite dead,
But for signs of life
Engraved into the snow.

Rachel Alban (13)
Polam Hall School

Summer

Sweet is the smell of the flowers,
Evergreen are the trees that stand high,
Warm is the delicate breeze,
Bold is the sky, the dome that covers us all
With bright, blinding stars
That look over us day after day.

Excited happiness is in us all
To enjoy this wondrous season.
Let us dance on the warm, soft soil;
Roll down the fragrant, grassy hills;
Play on the velvety, camel-coloured sand.

Listen to the peaceful music of the birds
And pick the succulent fruit from its dwelling,
Gaze at the scenery
And watch the clouds' shadows'
Leap about on the fells below,
Heed the wildlife,
See how they react to the marvellous weather -
We possess this season.

Kristina Gallagher (13)
Polam Hall School

Snow

S nowflakes falling
N ow it's all white
O n my house
W hat a nice sight
F alling from the midnight sky
L anding on the path while I
A m looking out my window clear
K eep hearing crunchy footsteps
E asily appear
S un has come, it's disappeared.

Ashleigh Williams (12)
Roseberry Sports & Community College

A Spell

We make spells
Until it smells
We add lots of stuff
Even if one of us goes in a huff

This is how it goes
Old biddies' toes
An eye of newt
An awful brute

My mam's hair
With no care
A lump of fat
With a hairy dog mat

My grandma's feet
A head of a sheep
This is all
Now we all fall

It's all in a hoop
We made our soup.

Mark Lynn (12)
Roseberry Sports & Community College

Winter

Silver moon
In the noon
Pure white snow
Sun's its foe

Snowmen standing tall and proud
Children playing, shouting loud
Snow-topped trees like cakes
What fun winter makes!

Laura Pearson (12)
Roseberry Sports & Community College

A Beautiful World

Big, thick branches with scrawny fingers,
Reach up and grab the blue, frosty sky,
The golden leaves that fall off the trees,
Flutter and glide by,
Crisp, crack and *crunch* the leaves go,
As people walk by,
Each of them fascinated by the blue, frosty sky.

Look! There's a stream,
That sparkles and shivers in the golden sunlight,
People that slip in get a bit of a fright,
Bubble, splish, splosh and *splash* is the sound it makes,
While the moon lights up a beautiful world,
Looking for wonders it might make.

The rain falls like there is no end,
While animals look for a new friend,
The cobwebs are jewelled in the colours of the rainbow,
My nose and fingers are easily cold though,
When the rain goes the scent lingers,
The smell of pine on the tips of my fingers.

Sarah-Lee Gordon Pearse (12)
Roseberry Sports & Community College

My Baby Brother

He's small, he's round,
He bounces up and down.
He's cuddly, he's cute,
He chews on my dad's boot.

He's destructive, he's a mess maker,
He's annoying, he's a toy breaker.
He's amusing, he's entertaining,
He's loud, he's frustrating.

Laura Ames (12)
Roseberry Sports & Community College

Iraq

Iraq,
Iraq means war,
Iraq means fear,
Iraq means fright,
Iraq is our soldiers having to fight.

Iraq,
Iraq means death,
Iraq means destruction,
Iraq means depression,
Iraq, it was.

Iraq,
Iraq is peace,
Iraq is love,
Iraq is children playing with doves,
Iraq, it will be.

James Gibbs (13)
Roseberry Sports & Community College

I Had a Wiggly Tooth

I had a wiggly tooth
It hurt by day
It hurt by night
So I went to the dentist
Who said, 'In time
It will fall out and you'll be fine.'

The next day out it fell
I was so happy, all was well
On going to bed under the pillow it went
Where it turned into a pound
Which has been long since spent!

Lyndsey Brown (13)
Roseberry Sports & Community College

Hallowe'en

Hallowe'en, a frightening time,
A holiday with a nasty rhyme,
The ghosts, the witches,
The vampires and bats,
The monsters, the zombies,
The witch's black cat,
All come out on that
Hallowe'en night,
To give us all a big, nasty fright!
So next time you think of walking the streets,
Or going outside to play trick or treat,
Think of the monsters, vampires and bats,
And stay inside away from the rats.

Sophie Short (11)
Roseberry Sports & Community College

Friends

Friends are weird, friends are cool,
Always acting like a fool.
Have a laugh every day,
Always friendly, something to say.
In a huff, sometimes sad,
Being silly, always mad.
In a strop, but still my friends,
Time to make up, every thing mends.
But still around with our groovy trends!

Marie Forster (12)
Roseberry Sports & Community College

Crushes

Crushes are really weird,
People can't say what they really feel.
So I began to wonder
Why are crushes real?

Why did God create them?
When people really feel
Like cupid's shooting arrows
Why are crushes real?

Natasha Jayne Scott (12)
Roseberry Sports & Community College

Wake Up

One thing that I terribly hate
Is having to wake up at eight
On Saturday, Sunday and Monday as well
it is a pain, worse than Hell.

My mum shouts from the bottom of the stairs
'Get up you lazy bear'
A few minutes later I jump out of bed
brush my teeth, wash my hands and get ready as well.

I jump down the stairs as fast as a hawk
Eat my breakfast
And off to school I go.

I jump into the car
And around the corner we speed
Just in time for the bell
What a relief.

I hate getting up on Saturday, Sunday and Monday as well
Believe me, it is pain worse than Hell.

Jennifer Anderson (11)
Roseberry Sports & Community College

Chocolate

C hocolate is my favourite treat
H urry down to the corner shop
O ne by one I search through the shelves
C adbury's is the one I chose
O range flavour I really like
L ick my lips with pleasure
A fter all the bars have gone
T ime to put away all the wrappers
E njoy your chocolate, it's the best!

Chloe Williams (11)
Roseberry Sports & Community College

Kittens

Kittens are so sneaky,
They're cuddly and ever so cheeky,
I love them because they're caring,
They sit with little eyes glaring,
Their hearts are filled with love,
Watching me from up above.

Natalie Duncan (12)
Roseberry Sports & Community College

Autumn Time

Autumn time is really fun
With golden trees and watery sun
Autumn time brings falling leaves
Moving around in the gentle breeze
Autumn time brings darker nights
Country walks and conker fights
Autumn time brings sparkling rain
With dreams of far-off sunny Spain.

Anna Widdrington (11)
Roseberry Sports & Community College

A Cold, Frosty Day

Frosty fields covered with snow,
The green fields no longer show.
The trees swift and howl left to right,
Giving every animal a warning fright.
The branches break and crash to the ground,
They fall and shatter with a massive pound.
Birds sit with their babies and squirm,
Mothers looking out to find a worm.
Rabbits hunt and find winter feasts,
But they can only find the least.
Deer run and get caught in the frost,
All of their younger ones getting lost.

Kate Atkinson (11)
Roseberry Sports & Community College

My Hamster Hamish

My hamster Hamish is one of my best friends,
He is as agile as can be,
When he climbs to the top of his cage
And gnaws at his bars,
It is his attempt to break free.

My hamster Hamish is as cute as can be,
He is coloured golden and white,
He is curled up asleep for most of the day,
But has lots of fun at night.

My hamster Hamish is never apart from me,
We love to play together,
Sometimes he can be a mischievous little chap,
But he will be in my heart forever.

Alex Young (11)
Roseberry Sports & Community College

Our Astounding Planet

The Earth is a great round rock
Floating in the middle of space
But it is quite different
In this particular case
There are deep, long oceans
Full of liveliness
Stretching as far as the eye can see
And if you look up
Into the big blue sky there is a sun
Staring right back at me
There are little things like ants
That scuttle across the floor
And there are bigger things like lions
That run and crouch and roar
There are all different countries that
Stretch across the Earth
And all the time there are people laughing
And women giving birth
So people say that it is a little pinprick
In the big black sheet of night
But there are always creatures on that pinprick
Trying with all their might!

Andrew Lough (13)
Roseberry Sports & Community College

Jealousy

Jealousy is an emotion,
We all have to bear,
It's the green-eyed monster,
Without a care.

                      It enters our minds,
                      It makes us see red.

We say awful things,
We later dread.

                      We try to control it,
                      It damages your health,
                      But the only one who
                      Suffers is yourself.

Yasmine Khalifa (14)
Roseberry Sports & Community College

Boys Are Boys

Boys are boys
You can't help but love them.
But they are such a pain.
And never listen to what you are saying.

Boys are boys
In trackies and trainers.
Listening to the music in their room.
It just sounds like *boom, boom, boom!*

Boys are boys
They've got girls in a trance.
When going to discos
They watch them dance.

Boys are boys
We can't help the way they are!

Natalie Thompson (13)
Roseberry Sports & Community College

Sorrow

Sorrow.

Sorrow depresses the soul,
Sorrow rips out your heart and stamps on it.

Sorrow is the darkest black,
Sorrow is as rough as glass paper,
Sorrow is as sharp as a Samurai sword.

Sorrow is to be hurt because of your culture,
Sorrow is to be bullied,
Sorrow is to leave good friends,
Sorrow is the coldest and hardest day.

Sorrow.

Brian Ashman (13)
Roseberry Sports & Community College

The Bully

Why are you such a bore?
On detention more and more
Why every day do you stand
And stare, call us names
And pull our hair?

Why is it you never tried
To know the hurt we feel inside?
Because I think that in the end
You could still be our friend.

Paul Hunt (13)
Roseberry Sports & Community College

Days

Days go by fast and slow
They pass us quick
We sometimes wonder where they go
They pass slowly
We wonder when they will end
Things can happen we never know
We always think the night before
Is the next day going to be bad or good?
We never know.

Thomas Owers (13)
Roseberry Sports & Community College

War

War is hell
Hell is fighting, bombs and explosions
War is our enemy
Our enemy are people who want what they can't have
War is poverty
Poverty is hunger, death and disease
War is death, murder, killing
Death is being shot
Death is being caught in a crossfire
War is people dying
Dying is when you are finally at peace
War is children crying
Children crying is when they are homeless
War is the world's worst nightmare
The world's worst nightmare is countries
Destroyed and governments demolished
War is pain
Pain is death, hunger and disease
War is not a game.

Dayne Nicholson (14)
Roseberry Sports & Community College

Disappointment

Disappointment is where you try and help someone
and they push you away
Disappointment is when you love someone
and they don't love you
Disappointment is when someone's not your friend
Disappointment feels like you've been hit in the face
Disappointment is when your girlfriend leaves you
Disappointment is when you get told off
Disappointment is like the colour black
Disappointment is when people lie
Disappointment is where people tease you
Disappointment is a really bad feeling
Disappointment is something bad that has happened.

Scott Harrison (13)
Roseberry Sports & Community College

Love

Love is a warm feeling
That bubbles inside,
Love is something you
Just can't hide.

Love is something special
That you must treasure,
Love is something you
Just can't measure.

Love; it grows day by day,
Love is something
You can't lock away

You can't deny love - if it is real,
You've just got to let it out
And show what you feel.

Lauren Bates (13)
Roseberry Sports & Community College

My Sister

My sister is a pain,
She drives me insane,
She nicks all my stuff,
And walks in when I'm in the buff.
She pinches my clothes,
Which will not fit as she grows.
'Mum!' I shout, 'my sister's a pain.'
What I would give for a minute's peace.
I know she could play with my niece,
But that's not so.
Mum said, 'No she can't go.'
Oh no, my sister is such a pain!

Kayleigh Worrall (13)
Roseberry Sports & Community College

Valentine's

Valentine's, Valentine's
    Smell the love
Valentine's, Valentine's
    See the doves.

Valentine's, Valentine's
    Pick a rose
Valentine's, Valentine's
    Pick a pose.

Valentine's, Valentine's
    Find the smell
Valentine's, Valentine's
    A broken spell.

Laura McFarling (11)
Roseberry Sports & Community College

A Birthday Poem

Remember the times
We'd laugh in the sun
Playing games together
We had so much fun.

Now that we're older
These things that we share
Become very special
And show us we care.

So let's have a party
Let me share that with you
We'll drink to each other
But you're on your own if you spew!

Helen Shaw (13)
Roseberry Sports & Community College

Christmas Poem

Christmas is such a joyful time,
To be funny you can mime.

Outside you're playing,
In the snow you're sleighing.

When you're out shopping,
Others are party popping.

It really is happy,
While partying your feet get tappy,
And your hands get clappy.

Christmas is such a wonderful time,
As I said, you can mime.

Callum McCutcheon (11)
Roseberry Sports & Community College

Fire, Fire

Fire, fire
Your desire
Shiny flame
Not a game
Creepy shimmer
Scary glimmer
Burning heat
Not neat
Flaming wood
It is good
Devil's furnace
Burn it, burn it
Burning bright
In the light
It's what I like
On Bonfire Night.

Fireworks popping
Bang! Bang! Bang!
Sparklers clicking
With a clang
Roman candles
Pop, pop, pop!
Rockets blasting
Up the top
Matches striking
Fsh, fsh, fsh
Air bombs banging
Spsh, spsh, spsh
Righteous rockets
Going bang
Lighters gassing
It's not lasting
If you like it
Dare a dare.

Callum Sharpe (12)
Roseberry Sports & Community College

My Poem

Unicycling is lots of fun
Especially eating a big cream bun!
Staying on is really hard,
Specially when it feels like you ride on lard.
On road, off road, in the air,
It makes everyone around you stare.
Big and small, back to front,
The whole thing is a great big stunt.

I practised hard when I was small,
Now I don't fall off at all.
I got the idea from my dad,
He can ride too, he's not half bad.
When I go to a circus convention,
I get a lot of crowd attention.
Sometimes they shout rude comments like,
'Can't you afford a proper bike!'

Jack Norwood (11)
Roseberry Sports & Community College

Stars

Stars are just figures in the sky,
But how brightly they shine is different,
It is God's creation of light in the night,
And shouldn't be tampered with.
But people didn't believe that,
So they put up lights instead.
Oh how it ruins the sky, the night, the stars.
It is so much nicer with the stars shining alone up in the night.
It's so much nicer and brighter than it is with lights.

Rebecca Simpson (11)
Roseberry Sports & Community College

I Love The Mighty Ducks

My favourite sport is ice hockey
My favourite team's the Ducks
I love the thrill of seeing them
Going for the puck.

As we shout for joy
Our brilliant goalie saves
While we're in the crowd we sit so proud
Doing the Mexican wave.

I like to see the goals
I love to see the fights
I think the Ducks are the best
I really hope I'm right.

Justine Ovington (12)
Roseberry Sports & Community College

The 11th Of September

R emember, remember the 11th of September,
E veryone was crying,
M any were dying,
E veryone remembers how this tragedy happened,
M any were sighing,
B ecause of this tragedy,
E veryone remembers,
R emember, remember the 11th of September.

R ubble and dirt was everywhere,
E very place was covered in dust,
M any people were saying goodbye,
E ven though they might be alive,
M ums and dads were horrified,
B ecause of what they'd seen and heard
E verything was ruined,
R escuing people for days and days.

    Remember.

Chloe Miles (11)
Roseberry Sports & Community College

Happy Poem

Happy is being with my mum
Happy is getting new clothes
Happy is lying in at weekends
Happy is not going to my dad's
Happy is going swimming with my friends
Happy is visiting my friends
Happy is going to my grandma's house
Happy is going on holiday
Happy is playing in the pool
Happy means having fun on Christmas Day
Happy is meeting my old friends from primary school and stuff
Happy means to me having fun and being joyful.

Gemma Piggford (11)
Roseberry Sports & Community College

What Is War?

War is guns shooting
And swords stabbing the enemy
War is innocent civilians being killed by bombs
Falling from the sky
War is a time of danger
Of battles and of death
War is the sign of no peace
The sign of anger and evil
War is two countries coming together
Unexpectedly and unwantingly
War is mines blowing up people by surprise
War is disaster
War is evil.

Benjamin Brown (12)
Roseberry Sports & Community College

Ice Cream

I love ice cream, loads of different flavours
So delicious, don't want to share with neighbours

It's so wet and cold
Far too cold to hold

In your ice cream you put flakes
Sometimes it can be in cakes

I love ice cream, loads of different flavours
So delicious, don't want to share with neighbours

If it's not in a cone
Some people tend to moan

Some ice cream is lush
Sometimes turns to mush

I love ice cream, loads of different flavours
So delicious, don't want to share with neighbours.

Emma Wilson (12)
Roseberry Sports & Community College

Winter

Winter, winter all around
I stop still and stare at the ground
What do I see, nothing but snow
I see that white, crispy, shiny glow
I love this cold winter phase
The frost and ice with a silky glaze -
But what I love best is the snow
The snow with the white, crispy, shiny glow.

Stephnie Coyle (13)
Roseberry Sports & Community College

Hallowe'en Is Nearly Here

Hallowe'en is nearly here,
Get ready for your fear.
Bats dart around the moonlit sky,
The moon lies very high.
Your mam and your dad might give you a sweet,
Knock at a door, they will give you a treat.
Hallowe'en night is very scary,
Monsters' feet are very hairy.
You go trick or treating all day,
Hallowe'en is nearly here.

Matthew Gray (11)
Roseberry Sports & Community College

Cat Poem

I have a cat called Lucy,
But she's not a very nice cat.
She's black and white with a little pink nose,
That's my cat Lucy.

She bites and scratches when in a mood,
That's my cat Lucy.
As I stroke her she licks my hand,
That's my cat Lucy.

She miaows when she wants to be fed,
That's my cat Lucy.
She brings back mice as a gift,
That's my cat Lucy.

She sits at the window like a statue,
That's my cat Lucy.
When I come home she purrs at my feet,
That's my cat Lucy, that's my nice cat Lucy.

Ashleigh McCluskey-Walke (11)
Roseberry Sports & Community College

Christmas Poem

Christmas Eve, an exciting night
I lie in bed and sleep I fight
I can smell the aroma of turkey cooking
I find myself at the window looking
At a dark, starry sky, waiting for Santa's sleigh
Thinking of all the great presents
I might get on Christmas Day!
I am cosy and warm yet my stomach feels sick
The excitement and hoping to see St Nick
I lie there endlessly counting sheep
Eventually I must have fallen asleep
I wake up early
Feel a weight at my feet
I hope it's my stocking, *yes!*
All full of sweets
I jump out of bed and shout, 'He's been!'
I wake Mum and Dad, they don't look so keen
I run down the stairs and fling open the door
A scream of delight, a laugh and a roar
As I tear open each present
I feel such joy
A wonderful time for every girl and boy
Every time I think about my great day
I wish time could stand still
And it was here to stay.

Scott Docherty (11)
Roseberry Sports & Community College

Animals Big, Animals Small

Animals big, animals small,
A little white mouse or a giraffe really tall.
All can be found all over the world,
Even under the sea or buried in sand.

Animals big, animals small,
A cat likes a mouse while a dog likes a ball.
Some live in a house, some live in a cage,
Some live with humans, whatever their age.

Animals big, animals small,
We could go on for hours trying to think of them all.
From a little white rabbit to a tiger standing tall,
There's animals big and animals small.

Kristina Stafford (11)
Roseberry Sports & Community College

Hallowe'en Night

On Hallowe'en
You should beware
Of ghosts and ghouls in the cold night air.

Screeches and screams throughout the night,
Everyone's in for a heck of a fright.

As the dead walk the Earth on October 31st,
Looking for blood and flesh to quench their thirst.

Bats fly through the air,
Rats scatter the pavements,
Witches and warlocks with evil entertainments.

As midnight approaches and the witching hour draws near,
We're all tucked up in bed away from our fear.

Hallowe'en has been and gone,
And I'm proud to say I have survived this one!

Anna Jobling (11)
Roseberry Sports & Community College

Favourite Things

Nice-smelling perfume
And songs with a nice tune
Cute mini dresses
And hair done in tresses
Snow goes in winter
As rain into spring
These are all of my favourite things

Snowmen and sleigh bells
And food with some nice smells
Dancing in tap shoes
And gossip and friends' news
Presents at Christmas
With bows and tied strings
These are all of my favourite things

White furry bunnies
And jokes that are funny
Views over mountains
And waterfall fountains
Birds flutter by
With brown-feathered wings
These are all of my favourite things.

Kristie Armstrong (12)
Roseberry Sports & Community College

Mother

M is for mam who I love and care for
O is for the other little things you give me
T is for tender love and care you give me
H is for the house you keep me in
E is for either way you love me so
R is for respect I give you.

Laura Alderson (11)
Roseberry Sports & Community College

Puppet Girl's War

She lives like a puppet,
The strings pulling at her heart,
Hiding from the world
The only one left.

Her joints becoming rusty,
Creaking as she creeps,
Her painted face still smiling,
Though deep inside she weeps.

She longs for her own freedom,
Away from wars of hell,
She peers through the curtains,
And hears the sirens roar.

Running from her death,
Imagining her fate,
She dodges a falling boulder,
But sadly it's too late.

That night when survivors came,
To search upon the ground,
Battered, cracked and broken,
The puppet girl was found.

Jasmine Mulligan (12)
Roseberry Sports & Community College

Friends

I love my friends,
They're always around,
They see through me like a sun through the clouds.
They comfort me when I am sad,
And cherish me when I am glad.
They give presents for birthdays,
And I return them with presents from holidays.
I don't know what I would do without my friends,
'Cause I know our friendship will never end.

Rachel Campbell (12)
Roseberry Sports & Community College

Golfer's Haiku

I love playing golf
I love the swish of the clubs
I hate the bad shots

I love playing off
The balls soar like aeroplanes
My clubs are my tools

I love playing golf
When I get a hole-in-one
The crowd chants my name.

Ben Johnson (12)
Roseberry Sports & Community College

Stupid Dare

I knew I was in for a really big scare,
When I agreed to do a horrible dare;
I had to go into a forest, dark and damp,
There wasn't a light, not even a lamp.
I walked and walked over and over,
While stroking my best dog Rover.

I looked at red eyes giving a stare,
I ran thinking it was a bear.
I saw a creature flying above,
I was hoping it was only a dove.
It wasn't, it wasn't, it was really bad,
I could tell it was really mad.
I ran, I ran, I had a scare,
I'm never accepting another dare.

Chris Smith (12)
Roseberry Sports & Community College

My Poem About A Poem

I told my mates I'd write a poem,
About a poem I told 'em.
How do you find all that rhyme?
Oh how this poem does shine.
My mates are gonna be stuffed,
I'm the one that's gonna be chuffed.

Here comes the second verse,
Now my mates will disperse.
They're so scared I'll win the bet.
They're trying to bribe me with their ket.
This poem business is quite easy,
All that food is making me queasy!

Now here comes the last few lines,
They're praying now in different shrines.
This poem might go in a book,
Then everyone can have a look.

Oh what a life I have, it's Heaven
This poem was written by Christopher Bevan,
Get in, I've won the bet,
They'll have to get me loads more ket.

Christopher Bevan (12)
Roseberry Sports & Community College

My Mates And Me

My time is so fun for me
It's all about my mates and me
Our time is when we're off school
We can just hang out, chill and be cool
It's better in the holidays
Cos we can just relax and laze
My time is so fun for me
It's all about my mates and me.

Carley Cockburn (12)
Roseberry Sports & Community College

My Sister

I have a new sis,
No more bliss.
We've made a game,
To choose a name.
Oh, can't you tell,
Nappies that smell,
Make babies that stink,
Need to be washed in the sink.
Night-time wakers,
Sleep breakers.
It won't be long,
Soon she'll be one.
She'll learn to walk,
Then to talk.
She'll run for miles,
And give lots of smiles.
Once she starts school,
She'll be ever so cool.
She'll meet girls and boys,
And makes lots of noise.

Kimberley Bell (12)
Roseberry Sports & Community College

School Buses

School buses I hate,
Because they make me late.
Always last at the gate,
Never arrive before half-eight.

When the bus is red,
I just want to go to bed.
When the bus is yellow,
I want to bellow.

Ryan Mowbray (11)
Roseberry Sports & Community College

Without You

You are my everything
My friend, my love
You are more magnificent
Than a flying white dove.

My love for you
Is ever so strong
Just like a melody
In the most beautiful song.

I enjoy the times
When you are near
When I am with you
I feel no fear!

You are my reason
For hanging on
Without you
I would be gone.

Daynor Dockery (12)
Roseberry Sports & Community College

Mable And Her Puppies

I woke up, I heard a squeak
There was Mable on my fleece
Six little puppies all asleep
Then woke up wanting to eat.

Me wandering round
Biting my nails
Mable running wild
Wagging her tail.

When I put Mable back to sleep
I heard the puppies starting to weep
Shh, shh, shh.

Natalie Barker (11)
Roseberry Sports & Community College

Babies

Babies, babies grow in your tummy,
Babies, babies suck on a dummy.
Babies, babies cry all day,
Babies, babies like to play.
Babies, babies eat their food,
Babies, babies can get in a mood.
Babies, babies play with toys,
Babies, babies make loads of noise.
Babies, babies, what's your name?
Babies, babies *are a pain!*

Sally Hunter (13)
Roseberry Sports & Community College

Remember The 5th

Fireworks fizzing into the sky,
Fireworks banging up above,
Fireworks spinning and puffing and smoking,
Fireworks being watched by everyone.

Bonfire growing tall,
Bonfire blazing and hot,
Bonfire feeding on the wood,
Bonfire reaching the sky to come back again.

Sparklers all different colours,
Sparklers bright and beautiful,
Sparklers lighting up the night,
Sparklers loved by children big and small.

Bonfire Night with fireworks bright,
Bonfire Night with children amazed,
Bonfire Night with petrified animals kept indoors,
Bonfire Night loved by all.

Donna Ashurst (12)
Roseberry Sports & Community College

Football Is The Best!

Football is bright,
And exciting too,
When you score,
You jump for joy,
And when you win,
You feel proud with your effort,
Football is the best!

Football is crazy,
But rough too,
When you get fouled,
Your manager goes mad,
And when you lose,
You take it seriously,
Football is the best!

Matthew Soulsby (11)
Roseberry Sports & Community College

Fool

I hate school
'Cause I'm a fool
Can't even add a simple sum
No wonder people say I'm dumb.

I also hate getting a detention
Well, I should pay attention
I like PE, it makes me smile
But I hate running a few miles.

I like getting out of school
But I think . . . *why smile, I'm a fool.*

Carl Gill (12)
Roseberry Sports & Community College

Inside The Tiger's Stripe

Inside the tiger's stripe, the pitch-black night
Inside the pitch-black night, the hidden forest
Inside the hidden forest, the tiger's jaw
Inside the tiger's jaw, the tapir's cry
Inside the tapir's cry, the watery grass
Inside the watery grass, the tiger's nose
Inside the tiger's nose, the scent of a fern
Inside the scent of a fern, the leafy forest
Inside the leafy forest, the tiger's eye
Inside the tiger's eye, the glimpse of a deer
Inside the glimpse of a deer, the rocky mountain
Inside the rocky mountain . . . tiger's feet.

Daniel Ross (11)
Roseberry Sports & Community College

Untitled

I stand at the station as quiet as can be,
I'm waiting for my train on platform three.
I check my watch, it's ten-past eight,
Then I hear an announcement to say it's running late.
My train arrives and I find my seat,
Along comes refreshments and I pick something to eat.
I begin to feel sleepy so I have a short nap
When I awake I take a look at my map.
I start to make plans and map out my day,
I'll show them to Will and see what he has to say.
My journey over, I've arrived on time,
I check my watch and it's quarter to nine.
I wait on my platform looking forward to the day,
I hear my name being called by my friend coming my way.

Ashton Carter Ridgway (11)
Roseberry Sports & Community College

Shopping

>Here and there from store to store,
>Buying, buying, still want more.

Bags are heavy, purses with money,
I have to spend, it's just so funny.

>I've bought enough, but I can't stop
>I'm telling you, I'll shop till I drop!

Chester, the Metro, Eldon Square
I've always got money I need to spare.

>Clothes, sweets, lovely stuff
>I buy them all and I'm just so chuffed.

You'll never believe the fun I've had
Running in shops, I might go mad!

>But at the end of the day my purse is empty
>It's just as well, because I've bought plenty!

Katie Pearson (12)
Roseberry Sports & Community College

Opposites

A nger is annoyance and pain,
N astiness is what anger causes,
G uilt, jealousy and rage,
E ager to cause pain to other people,
R ealising how stupid you've been.

L ove is joy and emotion,
O ptional who you feel this for,
V ery easy to fall in love,
E ager to see this person again.

Abigail Forster (11)
Roseberry Sports & Community College

Cookie, What A Cat!

Long black fur with tints of ginger,
Eyes that shine in the dark like glitter.
Bright green eyes yet transparent like glass,
Her big black pupils darting so fast.

Dainty paws, dainty all together,
Always so frisky despite the weather.
Like all cats she's always aware,
A cat so special, a cat so rare.

Get out her toy mouse and she dances across the carpet,
She stalks her toy mouse and pounces on it, yet still so quiet.
At the end of the day she loves a fuss,
What a cat, what a puss.

Holly Tallentire (12)
Roseberry Sports & Community College

Autumn, Winter And Spring

Autumn, winter and spring
Summer, summer it is hot
But winter is not
Eating ice cream all day
And going out to play
As winter is here
Summer will come next year
As we play in the snow
Winter will soon go
When spring will start
Flowers will come in March.

Daniel Howe (11)
Roseberry Sports & Community College

Winter

As morning breaks
Comes the crisp snowflakes
Winter winds blow
A great avalanche of snow.

Children come out to play
Having lots of fun today
When evening comes they have frostbite
And go in for the night.

Now come evening skies
Through which the robin flies
Its bright red chest
Is at its best.

Winter snow falls very slow
As families watch the evening show
It is the end of the day
Children plead for the snow to stay.

Paul William Franklin (11)
Roseberry Sports & Community College

My Friend

M e and my friend have fun
Y ou are always there for me, you're kind and make me happy

F riends never lie to each other
R ight on time to meet me after school
I go to my friend's on time and we have fun
E very day we think of each other
N ever fight and never argue
D ay after day we play!

Danielle Graham (11)
Roseberry Sports & Community College

Wonderful Bats

Vampires drink blood,
They fly around in the bitter cold,
They are blind and fearful,
They are scared and old,
They are vampire bats.

Vampire bats fly like a graceful swan,
Their echoes are as quiet as a newborn mouse,
They fly through forests and farmlands,
They are vampire bats.

Vampire bats protect their young,
They teach them how to fly,
They teach them to listen to echoes,
They are vampire bats.

Vampire bats live in dark caves,
They sleep during the day and fly by night,
Now they say goodnight for now,
Until they rise again.

Sally Ann Rawlinson (12)
Roseberry Sports & Community College

Fireworks

F lying high,
I diots get hurt,
R oam the sky,
E yes are dazzled by the lights
W onderful and amazing
O ne after another the dazzling colours fill the sky
R eds, purples and pinks dance in the sky
K illing the stars
S parklers drawing patterns in the air.

Jamie Patterson (11)
Roseberry Sports & Community College

Silver Seal

Silver seal on a beach,
Many secrets not to teach.
All alone, safe and sound,
Like a reflecting sand mound.

He likes to lie and sulk,
Sunbeam bounces off his bulk.
With a tremendous roar,
Seagulls started to soar.

Fur like sun lotion,
He waddles to the ocean.
Through a reef,
To the soundless abyss.

Dale Bruce Purvis (12)
Roseberry Sports & Community College

Football Fan

F antastic football, fabulous
O ozy dribbling by Henry
O n the ball
T errific skill
B allistic, chaos and fighting
A ndy Griffin hits it up
L aughing and excitement
L ua Lua does his flips

F ootball crazy
A mazing, skilful players
N ever to be ignored.

Christopher Waistell (11)
Roseberry Sports & Community College

Alone

Down in the deep dark forest,
Where they said you shouldn't go,
Something moves amongst the trees,
I've seen it, I should know.

Around the trees it lurches about,
Waiting for you to go,
For this foul demon is scared of you,
I've seen it, I should know.

I've seen the way it shuffles,
It's trying not to show,
That it's a lonely creature,
I've seen it, I should know.

It wades down near the waterside,
To watch the river flow,
And then it disappears,
I've seen it, I should know.

It used to walk around at night,
Although moving very slow,
It used to live in the deep dark forest,
I've seen it, I should know.

Stephen Lough (12)
Roseberry Sports & Community College

Bullies

We find bullies everywhere,
We find them here, here and there,
A bully can be a boy or a girl,
Mess with them and they'll make you whirl.

Try to keep away, they're up to no good,
They'll dunk you and drown you in black, filthy mud.
Let it be said they're nasty and mean,
Make sure you're nice but not very keen!

Sophie Harkness (11)
Roseberry Sports & Community College

Love And Cherish

L is for loneliness that soon disappears
O is for others who share your life
V is for a vase that you put red roses in
E is for the easy path to choose

C is for when you cherish each other
H is for hatred which becomes forgotten
E is for everything that falls into place
R is for respect that you give to each other
I is for I who will take care of you
S is for sharing your relationship
H is for healthiness that we wish people to have.

Stephanie Carr (11)
Roseberry Sports & Community College

Who Is It?

Someone crawling
Someone sneaking
Someone killing
Who is it?

Someone sleeping
Someone snoring
Someone waking
Who is it?

Someone staring
Someone glaring
Someone murdering
Who is it?

Christopher Twycross (12)
Roseberry Sports & Community College

My Unreliable Friends

It seems as though my friends are nasty to me,
Just me, nobody else, just me.
This is why:
My friends are never next to me,
They never ring or call on me,
They always seem to ignore me,
So why must it rain on me?
Why are they cruel to me?
Why are they cruel only towards me?

It seems as though they are nasty to me,
Nobody else, but just to me.
This is also why:
They hang with girls, not me,
They hang with each other, not me.
They hang in the park, without me,
They have fun, without me.
These are my unreliable friends,
No one else's, just mine,
But I want to know,
Why they do it to me?
Why . . . ?

James Miller (12)
Roseberry Sports & Community College

Disappointment

Disappointment is waking up and realising it's Monday
Disappointment is walking to school in the pouring rain
Disappointment is walking into the freezing classroom
Disappointment is when I am walking into the class
                              and my friend isn't there
Disappointment is when I have to go to bed at 11pm!

Grant Stephenson (11)
Roseberry Sports & Community College

The Lonely Forest

The lonely forest stares up to the dark sheet that is night,
It really is a sobbing sight,
To see something so beautiful cry,
The leaves like tears falling from the trees,
Torn swiftly in the sky,
The trees become decrepit beasts,
Now snarling at the night,
Now fearfully look at them,
And get a shuddering fright.

Fiona Alyson Lane (12)
Roseberry Sports & Community College

My Hobbies

There are lots of things I like to do,
Play football and on the PS2.
I'm always on FIFA 2003,
Then I go downstairs and on the PC.

I have a game of basketball,
I play table tennis in the main hall.
I love to have a game of cricket,
I always get at least one wicket.

I always have a game of tennis,
On the court I'm a real menace.
Me and my friends go up to Lumley,
Just to have a game of rugby.

I sometimes have a walk to Chester,
And get the bus back, that's much better.
So these are some things I always do,
And I just felt like sharing them with you.

Tom Charlton (11)
Roseberry Sports & Community College

Boys, Boys, Boys

Boys are always shouting,
Boys are always rude,
Boys are always playing football,
When they're in the nude.

Boys are always nasty,
Boys don't really care,
When they get home,
They cuddle their teddy bear.

Boys are always dirty,
Boys roll in mud,
Boys never do,
What they really should.

Boys are always naughty,
Boys like their cigarettes,
Boys never like to know they're wrong,
And never seem to regret.

Sarah Davison (12)
Roseberry Sports & Community College

Feelings

A part of me feels lost inside,
A part of me just wants to hide.
The icy wind, a knock at the door,
A part of me just can't be alone.

A part of me feels alive,
A part of me just can't survive.
Shifting shadows, the moon shines bright,
A part of me quivers with fright.

But most of the time I'm happy,
And very rarely sad,
Because I'm one of those people
Who always wants to be glad.

Harriet Middleton (12)
Roseberry Sports & Community College

Blue Is . . .

Blue is a clear sky,
Blue is a blueberry in a pie,
Blue is a school blazer,
Blue is your brother's razor,
Blue is a library book never returned,
Blue is the water when your fingers are burned,
Blue is a car turning a bend,
Blue is a way of saying, 'The End.'

Thomas Bates (12)
Roseberry Sports & Community College

Dogs

A dog is a pal,
All spotty and patched.

A dog is a mate,
Waiting to welcome you when you're late.

A dog is a friend,
With you till the end.

A dog is a buddy,
Begging for its bone.

A dog is a lark,
Soaring to catch frisbees down in the park.

A dog is a guard,
Protecting your house from the yard.

I am the owner,
Loving it with pride.

Jonathan Brown (12)
Roseberry Sports & Community College

Yellow

Yellow is the sun shining,
Yellow are the petals of the daffodils
On the kitchen window sill,
It's the colour of my hair,
Of something I'd wear.

It's the colour of sand,
As it trickles through my fingers,
On a hot summer's day
For me,
It's Miss D's classroom wall,
It's my baby cousin's ball.

Yellow is a happy colour,
Of sun and children playing,
Yes, I think
Yellow's my favourite of all!

Georgia Gibson (12)
Roseberry Sports & Community College

Black, Black, Black

Black is a scream, a cry out for help,
Black is a secret, deep and dark.
Black is a child, lost and lonely,
Black is a tornado destroying the Earth.
Black is like a hissing snake,
Black is like a long-lost friend.
Black is a baby away from its mother,
Black is an angry storm . . .
   Black.

Sarah Harris (13)
Roseberry Sports & Community College

I Want World Peace

For my birthday,
I don't want a thing,
A bike,
A phone,
Or a diamond ring.

I don't want money
To spend all day,
A DVD or Walkman,
For my music to play.

I don't want a party,
For everyone to laugh,
I don't want bubbles,
To go in my bath.

What I want,
Lies deep within,
World peace for all,
Anything else is a sin.

Hannah Livesey (12)
Roseberry Sports & Community College

Morning

M is for midnight, passing over the daylight sky
O is for the opening of a new day
R is for rising of the morning sun
N is for the night when the stars shine bright
I is for interest of the moon and stars at night
N is for nocturnal creatures stalking the Earth
G is for glittering frost on the dewed grass.

Lynne Eason (12)
Roseberry Sports & Community College

Sisters

Fighting,
Screaming,
Naughty,
Opposites,
Name-calling,
That's what makes sisters.

Talking,
Laughing,
Fun,
Being there,
Listening,
That's what makes sisters.

Having fun,
Playing together,
Helping,
Mischief,
Sticking together,
That's what makes sisters.

When it all comes down to it,
I'm glad she's my sister.

Lauren Patterson (11)
Roseberry Sports & Community College

What Is Black?

Black is a walking killing machine,
It feels all cold and rough,
It sounds like a demon in the dark,
Screaming and shouting.
It smells like a decaying beast,
It looks like a mass murderer,
It tastes like a rotten egg sandwich.

Black strolls along in the night,
Frightening and making people lonely,
Black is senseless,
It doesn't care what it does.

Blackness has no heart.

Black is teeth decaying,
Black is shame,
Black is the sour milk on your cereal,
Black is the cut on your knee.

Black is death.

Michael Miley (13)
Roseberry Sports & Community College

Brothers

Brothers are always there,
even though they act as if they don't care,
They help through the good and bad,
although they tend to make you mad.

Brothers are crazy,
although they can be lazy,
many are sporty,
but at school they may be naughty.

Football is a common sport to brothers,
they tend to compete with many others,
so be careful of brothers,
and watch you don't become one of their lovers.

Nicola Hoyle (14)
The Hermitage School

Patriot

I will charge the battlefield for glory and for God and
take the enemy to sword.

When the conflict is over we will say we have done well
with General Stone and Colonel Davis,
national heroes we will be.
With flowers and honours we will be greeted.

When we have all gone to God and been forgotten,
people will ask why we shot and why we stabbed.
For the glory of God and the good of man
Or the fullness of your wallet?

So you tell us if we are men or murderers,
Because war is hell and in God we trust.

Jake Rollings (15)
The Hermitage School

Parties

Parties!
Some are good,
Some are bad,
Some are happy,
Some are sad
A party's a party,
An excuse to get tarty,
The drink is great,
You end up in a state.

The next morning you wake,
You always have to take a shake,
Your head's always battered,
'Cause the night before you got ratted.

Until the next time you party again,
I can't walk, my feet are in pain!

Kate Pickard
The Hermitage School

Football

Football is good, football is bad,
Any other sport, you must be mad.
No matter what position you play,
You'll get a win, home or away.

The team you play on the day
Will be strong and fight you away.
If you defeat them they will cry,
So don't be mean, throw them a pie.

To the manager he wants a win
And the crowd want to chant and sing,
The team players want a goal,
To do this you need a soul.

So go and train for your team,
If you get picked, shout and scream.
When you make your debut the first thing they will say to you
Is, 'Don't be a fool, we know we can't lose.'

Ian Potts (15)
The Hermitage School

Guitars

My guitar is new and modern
It rocks my head just like my music.
It's an Ibanze's, the rockiest guitar I know.
It's blue metallic, the same as my free plecs.
My bridge is high with a low tone.
The neck is maple but my fret board is rosewood,
The head is long but the humbucker longer
As it's a double coil.
My life is smooth, just like my guitar.

Mark Ridley
The Hermitage School

Football

Football, football, it is fun,
You feel great when you have won,
It is fun when you play for a team
Especially when you win the Premier League.

Waiting nervously to be picked,
Playing up front, I hope I don't get kicked.
When you get picked you feel great,
I get the number eight.

Whistle blows game kicks off,
Nervous until you get a touch.
If you score a load of goals,
You can be like David Beckham, 'Golden Balls'.

Whistle blows, free kick outside the box,
Nasty tackle has ripped my socks.
Chipped free kick hits the bar,
Over the wall, smashes a car.

Ten minutes left, we get a pen,
I hope I don't hit the bar again,
Nil-nil, the pressure's on,
This last chance could be the one.

Left or right, which way to go?
The referee's whistle blows.
I go left, in it goes,
Hits the back of the net,
This makes me the hero.

I run to the corner and do a flip,
Luckily for me I don't snap my hip.
The final whistle blows, we feel great,
I go home to celebrate.

Michael Patterson
The Hermitage School

After The War With Iraq

I am an Iraqi civilian,
The war has ended,
I have just come out of a bomb shelter,
We have been in there for weeks.

I smell the air, it smells of smoke from the fires
caused by the battles,
I see people crying after losing their friends or relatives
who have been killed,
I also see the ruins of what has been my home, now all of it is
just rubble covered in dust.

I taste the dust in my mouth after it has been scattered everywhere
by the bombs.

I hear the mourning of a family who have found their son was killed
because he was caught in the gunfire.

I wish this had never happened.
I hope that nothing like this happens again.

Christopher Porter (15)
The Hermitage School

Ryan

*(This poem is dedicated to Ryan, my old horse
who had to be put down early last year. RIP, Ryan)*

This beautiful thing, he stood up proud,
his eyes, they sparkled and shone out loud,
his tail rippled and swished all day,
and in my heart this thing must stay,
for Ryan, he could not return,
for this poor thing had had his turn,
he served us well until he fell.
He's gone to Heaven, not to Hell
and there he'll rest, it's for the best,
we had to let him go.

Lauren Prout (15)
The Hermitage School

Stupid War

It's wrong, this war with Iraq,
Half the world leaders need the sack.
They say they're trying to free Baghdad,
But Bush just wants to raise the American flag.

I think this war is really bad,
It's just Tony's latest fad.
George Bush will lead us all to war
Tony Blair will crawl along the floor.

Our soldiers will die pair by pair,
It seems their leaders don't really care.
Every day war cries get loud,
Soon we will attack the Iraqi crowd.

His special forces and his tanks
They will clash with our flanks,
After war we will need to mourn,
I feel it will be a never-ending storm.

Jonathan Carter (15)
The Hermitage School

Friends

Friends are very helpful,
Friends are very kind,
Friends help you through tough times
And pick you up when you are down.

Friends can be very nice,
Friends can be very nasty,
Friends can treat you with respect
And sometimes treat you like you're dirt.

But my friends are not like that,
They are very helpful,
They are very kind,
They help me through tough times.

That is why they are my friends.

Toni Paget
The Hermitage School

Teenage Life

The girls want the boys,
the boys want the girls,
it's just what goes on in the world.

People here, people there,
and other people just don't care.

Hearts for hearts,
gold for gold,
a little secret I've been told.

Stay out late,
get a date,
then just chill with a mate.

This is life, so I'm told,
I'm glad that friendships are made of gold!

Parents go really mad
when their children are very bad.

Life's full of love,
life's full of hate
and then there're things you just can't take.

Salt for salt,
pepper for pepper,
life's a b*tch, it can only get better.

Kathryn Louise Rudd (15)
The Hermitage School

And Here I Am And Now I've Gone!

I have a big brother but I am the oldest,
I have a pet dog but he is not mine,
I am loved but people do not care,
And here I am and now I've gone.

I told a story but no one heard,
The night is here but the day hasn't begun,
I have no time but time to spare,
And here I am and now I have gone.

I have a life but no life to live,
I'm busy tomorrow but there is no tomorrow,
I'm with a mate but my mate is not here,
And here I am and now I've gone!

Claire Renneberg (14)
The Hermitage School

Friends

It's good to have such special friends to talk to when you're blue.
Life would just be sad if I never had them round,
They make things go right when everything goes wrong.
They always bring out the happier side of me.
I know very few like that, that's why they're my best friends.

There's one, she's wild and crazy,
And the others think she's hip,
And there's one more, she's fantastic,
But above all, they're all so great.

I've never had best friends so good,
They are the rarest in the world!

Emma Hall (15)
The Hermitage School

Why War?

War is fierce, war is mad,
War takes away the father I had.
Walking in rows, in their three,
Off to face their destiny.

As they look into the enemies' eyes,
There bodies suddenly become paralysed,
As it begins with a boom,
The soldiers' deaths begin to loom.

Doing what they can against the threat,
Not fighting at all is the best bet.
Coming home to where they belong,
Drinking their drinks, singing their song,
As they're given their medals for their loyalty,
They are honoured by the royalty.
But do they realise what it's caused?
The mourning behind closed doors.

Nobody wins wars,
There's only losers.

Andrew Graham (14)
The Hermitage School